Management Accounting
Techniques Workbook

AAT Level 3 Diploma in Accounting

© Sheriden Amos, 2022

Image of owl © Eric Isselée-Fotolia.com

Published by Osborne Books Limited
Tel 01905 748071, Email books@osbornebooks.co.uk, Website www.osbornebooks.co.uk

Printed and bound by Stroma Ltd, UK.

ISBN 978-1-911198-88-8

how to use this Wise Guide

This Wise Guide has been designed to supplement your Tutorial and Workbook. It has two main aims:

▪ to reinforce your learning as you study your course

▪ to help you prepare for your online assessment

This Wise Guide is organised in the specific topic areas listed on pages 4 to 6. These individual topic areas have been designed to cover the main areas of study, concentrating on specific areas of difficulty. There is also an index at the back to help you find the areas you are studying or revising.

The Owl symbolises wisdom, and acts as your tutor, introducing and explaining topics. Please let us know if he is doing his job properly. If you have feedback on this material, please email books@osbornebooks.co.uk.

Thank you and good luck with your study and revision.

Osborne Books

REVISION TIPS

*'OWL' stands for: **O**bserve **W**rite **L**earn*

There are a number of well-known ways in which you can remember information:

- *You can remember what it looks like on the page. Diagrams, lists, mind-maps, colour coding for different types of information, all help you **observe** and remember.*

- *You can remember what you **write** down. Flash cards, post-it notes around the bathroom mirror, notes on a mobile phone all help. It is the process of writing which fixes the information in the brain.*

- *You can **learn** by using this Wise Guide. Read through each topic carefully and then prepare your own written version on flash cards, post-it notes, wall charts – anything that you can see regularly.*

- *Lastly, give yourself **chill out** time, your brain a chance to recover and the information time to sink in. Promise yourself treats when you have finished studying – a drink, chocolate, a work out. Relax! And pass.*

list of contents

1 Management accounting

INTRODUCTION

This unit covers management accounting, which examines the costs that are incurred in organisations. It also describes the revenue (or income) that is generated and explains how decisions that affect profit (revenue minus costs) can be made.

why use management accounting?

Management accounting helps managers to:

- record, monitor and control costs
- plan for the future
- make decisions for the business

how does management accounting differ from financial accounting?

This unit concentrates on management accounting, as seen in the following diagram.

All accounting must be carried out with integrity.

	FINANCIAL ACCOUNTING	MANAGEMENT ACCOUNTING
Data used:	Financial transactions	Financial transactions and external information, eg inflation rates
Formats:	Financial Statements: profit or loss, financial position	Management reports
Focus:	Past events	Future planning
Purpose:	Assess financial performance	Assist decision-making, planning and control
Produced:	At the end of a financial period	During a financial period
Users:	External: suppliers, banks	Internal: by management

2 Classifying costs

WAYS TO CLASSIFY COSTS

There are four main ways that costs can be classified (divided up). Although at first this classification process can seem confusing, each method is logical and needs to be understood.

classification by element

There are three elements of cost as follows:

- **materials** – the physical stuff that is used to make things or provide services (eg rubber used to make tyres or detergent to clean windows)

- **labour** – the cost of employing people to do things (eg a machine operator or a salesperson)

- **expenses** – costs which are neither materials nor labour (eg rent or electricity)

classification by nature

The meaning of this term is not immediately obvious. It means dividing costs into **direct** costs and **indirect** costs.

■ **direct costs** are costs that can be identified directly with each unit of output – these costs can be traced straight to the things being made or the service being provided. Units of output are also known as 'cost units' – a car, a hair cut, a book.

Examples of direct costs include:

- the costs of materials used to make products
- the cost of paying the people who are 'hands on' and directly involved in the manufacture of a product

■ **indirect costs** are the other costs – those that cannot be identified directly with each unit of output. These are often costs incurred in order to help make various products or provide a range of services.

Examples of indirect costs include:

- the cost of factory supervisors
- the cost of insurance

Indirect costs are also known as **overheads**.

classification by function

Costs can also be classified according to the **function** of the part of the organisation, eg the department that incurs the cost.

The main functions normally used for classification are:

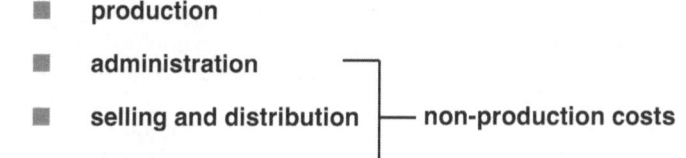

- **production**
- **administration**
- **selling and distribution** ⎤
- **finance** ⎦ — non-production costs

a note on function names:

- the function names are often the same as the department names

- 'production costs' may be referred to as 'factory costs'

- the administration, selling and distribution and finance costs may be referred to as 'warehouse' or 'office' costs

classification by behaviour

The idea of 'cost behaviour' refers to what happens to the total of any cost when the level of output changes.

The main types of **cost behaviour** are:

■ **fixed costs** – these do not change in total when output changes
Example: the cost of rent does not increase when output increases

■ **variable costs** – the total amount of a variable cost changes in proportion to the level of output
Example: the total cost of materials increases as output increases

■ **semi-variable costs** – these are a combination of fixed and variable costs
Example: the cost of electricity that includes a standing charge and a usage charge

■ **stepped fixed costs** – these costs are fixed within a range of output, but then 'step' up to a higher level for output in a higher range
Example: an additional supervisor is required when output increases above a certain level

3 Responsibility centres

WHAT ARE RESPONSIBILITY CENTRES?

These are used to enable managers to control the parts of the business for which they are responsible.

There are three types of responsibility centre. Each type is defined by what the centre does and what the manager can control.

types of responsibility centre

Responsibility centres are parts of the organisation where a particular manager has control.

The three types are:

- **cost centres** – where the manager just controls costs

  Example: an 'assembly' cost centre within the production function

■ **profit centres** – where the manager is responsible for both the revenue and the costs that result in profit

Example: the 'used cars' section of a car dealership; here the manager will be responsible for both buying and selling the used cars

■ **investment centres** – where the manager is accountable for the profit compared to the amount invested

Example: a single shop within a chain of shops; here the shop manager is responsible for making a profit and this is compared with the total investment in net assets in that shop

Responsibility centres can be used in conjunction with cost classification to analyse costs within management accounting systems.

The cost for each 'cost unit' can then ultimately be calculated.

4 Managing materials inventory

WHY CONTROL INVENTORY LEVELS?

Organisations should make sure that they hold an appropriate level of inventory of the various materials that they need.

If they hold too much inventory they risk storage and cash flow problems; too little and they may run out of inventory and bring production to a halt.

useful terminology

We need to understand the following terms so that we can use appropriate methods to control the level of inventories:

- **inventory buffer** – the extra amount of inventory that is held as a contingency (a 'reserve') – in case things do not go according to plan and there is the danger that inventory may run out

- **lead time** – the length of time between placing an order for more material and it actually arriving

- **re-order level** – when the inventory level drops to the re-order level it is time to place an order for more material

- **maximum re-order quantity** – the quantity of material that should be ordered each time (do not confuse this with the re-order level!)

- **maximum inventory level** – the largest amount of a material that will be held at any one time (it may be based on the capacity of the warehouse) – this will occur just after a delivery arrives

These terms are shown in the diagram below and their calculation on the pages that follow.

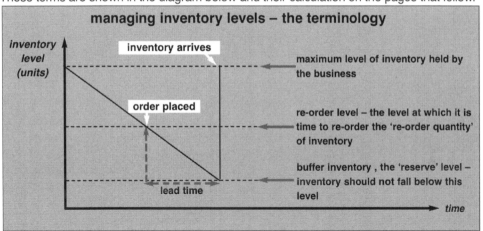

managing inventory levels – the terminology

inventory level (units)

inventory arrives

order placed

maximum level of inventory held by the business

re-order level – the level at which it is time to re-order the 're-order quantity' of inventory

buffer inventory , the 'reserve' level – inventory should not fall below this level

lead time

time

inventory calculations

■ **buffer inventory** is the minimum amount of inventory to be held, in case of emergencies; the buffer inventory is set by the purchasing or stores manager. It can be calculated as:

= re-order level – (average usage x average lead time)

■ **re-order level** is the units of inventory held when a re-order is required, so inventory is delivered prior to running out; it is:

= (average usage x average lead time) + buffer inventory

■ **maximum inventory level** is reached when a new delivery has just arrived; if this was ordered when the inventory had reached the re-order level it should arrive when the inventory reaches the 'buffer' point – the maximum inventory level is:

= buffer inventory + maximum re-order quantity

■ **re-order quantity** is decided by management as follows:

– the **minimum re-order quantity** will be just enough to avoid the inventory level going below the inventory buffer:

= average usage x average lead time

– the **maximum re-order quantity** will avoid the inventory level going over the maximum inventory level:
= maximum inventory level – buffer inventory

economic order quantity (EOQ)

This is the optimum (most economic) amount to order – to calculate it we need to know the following:

◼ **annual usage** – how many units are used each year (eg 20,000 units)

◼ **ordering cost** – the amount it costs to place one order (the administration cost), (eg £50)

◼ **inventory holding cost** – the cost of keeping one unit for one year (based on warehousing, insurance etc) (eg £2)

With this information we can calculate the EOQ as follows:

$EOQ = \sqrt{(2 \times annual\ usage \times ordering\ cost) \div inventory\ holding\ cost}$

Using the example figures quoted above this gives:

$EOQ = \sqrt{(2 \times 20{,}000 \times £50) \div £2}$

$= \sqrt{1{,}000{,}000}$

$= 1{,}000\ units$

5 Inventory valuation

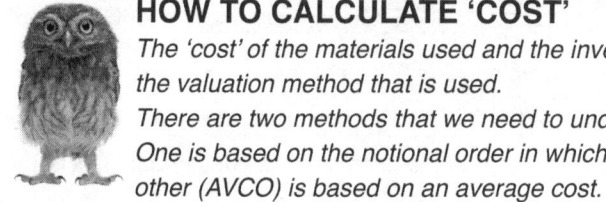

HOW TO CALCULATE 'COST'
The 'cost' of the materials used and the inventory remaining will depend on the valuation method that is used.
There are two methods that we need to understand and use for calculations. One is based on the notional order in which inventory is used (FIFO) and the other (AVCO) is based on an average cost.

outline of the two methods

■ **First In First Out (FIFO)** assumes that **the materials that arrive first are used first**, and so the valuation of the first issue of inventory is based on the cost of the first delivery. This means that it is possible that issues and balances of inventory at any one time can be split for valuation purposes and based on more than one price.

■ **Weighted Average Cost (AVCO)** is different from FIFO and LIFO – it does not assume any particular order of usage, but works out **an average cost based on all the deliveries**.

A weighted average cost (AVCO) is calculated each time more inventory arrives and this cost is used for both issues and balances until the next delivery arrives and the average is re-calculated.

You may well have studied inventory valuation in the previous level of your course and you should already be familiar with the way in which FIFO and AVCO work.

Note:

■ The actual order in which inventory is used does not have any impact on the choice of valuation methods.

■ When inventory valuations are used for financial accounting purposes, FIFO or AVCO can be used consistently to determine inventory value. The closing inventory value to use in the financial statements can then be determined by comparing this figure with 'net realisable value' and the lower figure is then used.

EXAMPLE – inventory valuation using FIFO

Inventory – Widgets (Medium)								
Date	Receipts			Issues			Balance		
	Qty	Cost Each £	Total Cost £	Qty	Cost Each £	Total Cost £	Qty	Cost Each £	Total Cost £
1 Nov							100	2.00	200
2 Nov	400	2.10	840				100	2.00	200
							400	2.10	840
							500		1,040
3 Nov				100	2.00	200			
				150	2.10	315	250	2.10	525
				250		515			
14 Nov	450	2.30	1,035				250	2.10	525
							450	2.30	1,035
							700		1,560
15 Nov				250	2.10	525			
				250	2.30	575	200	2.30	460
				500		1,100			

The calculations in this example are explained below.

EXAMPLE – inventory valuation using FIFO explained

The cost of **the issue of 250 units on 3 Nov** is worked out as follows:

100 units are matched with the opening balance of 100 units at £2.00 each	£200
150 units are matched with part of the receipt on 2 Nov at £2.10 each	£315
Total cost of issue	£515

This leaves the balance on 3 Nov matched with the remainder of the receipt on 2 Nov and valued at 250 x £2.10 = £525.

The cost of **the issue of 500 units on 15 Nov** is worked out as follows:

250 units are matched with the rest of the receipt on 2 Nov at £2.10 each	£525
250 units are matched with part of the receipt on 14 Nov at £2.30 each	£575
Total cost of issue	£1,100

This leaves the balance on 15 Nov matched with the remainder of the receipt on 14 Nov and valued at 200 x £2.30 = £460.

*Note that in an assessment you may need to carry out the calculations of the split valuations outside the table and only insert the **total** units and **total** cost for both issues and balances in the spaces provided.*

EXAMPLE – inventory valuation using AVCO

Inventory – Widgets (Medium)								
Date	**Receipts**			**Issues**			**Balance**		
	Qty	Cost Each £	Total Cost £	Qty	Cost Each £	Total Cost £	Qty	Cost Each £	Total Cost £
1 Nov							100	2.0000	200
2 Nov	400	2.10	840				500	2.0800	1,040
3 Nov				250	2.0800	520	250	2.0800	520
14 Nov	450	2.30	1,035				700	2.2214	1,555
15 Nov				500	2.2214	1,111	200	2.2214	444

The calculations in this example are shown on the next page. Note that the above example uses calculations to four decimal places. You will be told in your AAT assessment the number of decimal places that will be required. Note also that for both valuation methods, the total (cost of issues + valuation of final balance) is identical. This is an important feature and a useful check on calculations.

EXAMPLE – inventory valuation using AVCO

This method does not use a matching process, but instead calculates an average value per unit after each receipt and then uses that valuation for both issues and balances until the next receipt.

The **average value per unit after the receipt on 2 Nov** is calculated as:

Total cost (£200 opening balance + £840 receipt)	= £1,040
£1,040 divided by total units (100 + 400 = 500)	= £2.0800 per unit

This is used to value both the issue on 3 Nov, and the balance on 3 Nov.

The **average value per unit after the receipt on 14 Nov** is calculated as:

Total cost (£520 previous balance + £1,035 receipt)	= £1,555
£1,555 divided by total units (250 + 450 = 700)	= £2.2214 per unit

This is then used to value the issue and balance on 15 Nov, and also any further issues and balances until a further receipt arrives.

implications of the valuation method used

Because the cost of materials used is a deduction in the calculation of profit (revenue – cost of sales), the choice of valuation method will have an impact on recorded profits. Remember:

- if the cost of issues is higher (and the value of remaining inventory therefore lower) the profit will be lower, but . . .

- if the cost of issues is lower (and the value of remaining inventory therefore higher) the profit will be higher

In times of inflation (rising costs) the impact of valuation methods will be as follows:

- **FIFO** will result in higher values for remaining inventory and therefore **higher recorded profits and higher tax charges**

- **AVCO** will smooth out some of the highs and lows of profit or loss so taxes will also be smoothed

If there are generally falling prices then the valuation method will of course have the opposite effect to the above. Remember that once an inventory valuation method has been chosen, it must be applied consistently.

inventory valuation – summary

	FIFO	AVCO
principles	issues matched with earliest receipts in time order	no issue matching – weighted average cost calculated after each receipt
uses	management accounts and financial accounts	management accounts and financial accounts
effects of inflation (rising prices)	higher recorded inventory valuation and higher profits	the averaging process will reduce and smooth out the wider variations in inventory valuation and in profit or loss caused by inflation or deflation
effects of deflation (falling prices)	lower recorded inventory valuation and lower profits	

6 Labour costs

CALCULATING LABOUR COSTS

In this AAT unit you will need to know how to calculate employee pay. There are three main calculations involved: payment of basic pay, overtime, and bonuses. The actual calculations are quite straightforward, but understanding exactly what is required by the assessment tasks can provide a challenge!

the three types of employee pay

- **basic rate of pay** is the rate (usually hourly) that is paid for the normal hours of work

- **overtime** (time in excess of normal working hours) is often paid at a higher rate – this may be expressed in terms of the basic rate (for example, 'at time and a half') or as a 'premium' – an extra bit – which is added to the basic rate (for example, a premium of £8 per hour is added to a basic rate of £16 per hour to give a total overtime rate of £24 per hour)

- **bonuses** may be paid for production in excess of a stated level – this can be an individual bonus (for individual performance), or a group bonus that is worked out on the performance of a group and shared between the individuals

---

EXAMPLE – using basic pay and overtime

A company pays its production workers a basic rate of £16 per hour and a premium for any overtime work of £8 per hour. During the first week of November the employees worked 630 hours which included 80 overtime hours.

There are two alternative ways of carrying out the calculation of total pay:

1. Basic hours (550 x £16 = £8,800) + overtime hours (80 x £24 = £1,920)
   Total cost = £10,720

2. Total hours at basic rate (630 x £16 = £10,080) + overtime premium (80 x £8 = £640)
   Total cost = £10,720

The method to be used will depend on the exact requirements of the task – you may need to insert specific figures when you work out the answer.

EXAMPLE – using bonuses

A company pays its production workers a basic rate of £16 per hour and a premium for any overtime work of £8 per hour. A production target is set at 4 units for each labour hour worked (including overtime hours). A group bonus is payable of £1.50 per unit produced in excess of the target. During the first week of November the employees worked 630 hours which included 80 overtime hours. The production level achieved was 2,700 units.

The calculation is shown below on the left and the workings are on the right:

Basic pay (including basic hours for overtime)	£10,080	*(630 x £16)*
+ Overtime premium	£640	*(80 x £8)*
+ Bonus payment	£270	*[2,700 – (630 x 4) units] x £1.50*
= Total cost	£10,990	

Note how the second method from the previous page (basic pay and overtime) is used here to work out the answers.

●●●●●●●●●●●●●●●●●●●●●●●●●●●●●

labour costs – direct or indirect?

The rule that **direct costs** are those that can be identified directly with each unit of output applies to labour costs. Therefore . . .

- the pay for **production operatives** will generally be classed as **direct costs**

- the pay for **production supervisors** and **non-production employees** will be treated as **indirect costs**

But . . .

- **overtime premium** paid to **production operatives** is usually classed as an **indirect cost** because it is not normally linked to specific units but spread over all output along with other overheads

- an exception to this would be if the overtime was a requirement of a specific urgent job and then the premium would be a legitimate **direct cost** of that job

Also . . .

- **idle time** is when a worker is paid but is not engaged in production work (eg when machinery breaks down or the employee undergoes training). For production workers, **idle time** is also usually treated as an **indirect cost**

7 Dealing with overheads

MATCHING OVERHEADS TO OUTPUT

The challenge here is to spread the cost of overheads fairly over the output of the organisation. The first three steps are explained in this chapter, with the final step – absorption – explained in the following chapter. The overall process will enable you to work out the amount of indirect costs that relate to each unit produced.

the steps in the process

The diagram below illustrates all four steps involved:

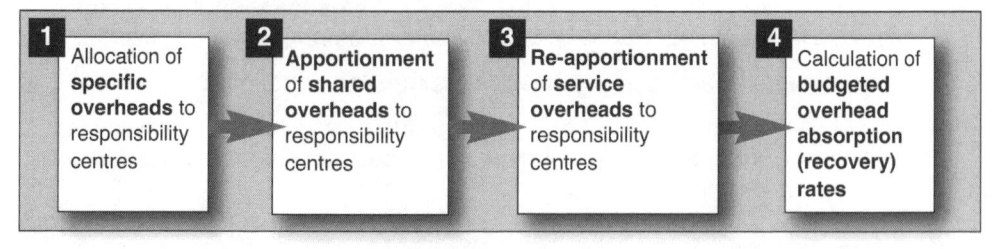

the steps explained

These steps are used to analyse budgeted production overhead costs so that a **budgeted overhead absorption (recovery) rate** can be calculated. This can then be used to provide a value for indirect costs in products and services under absorption costing.

Step 1: allocation of specific costs to responsibility centres

- Some indirect costs clearly relate to only one responsibility centre – for example, the salary of a supervisor in the packing department.

- These costs are allocated direct to the relevant centre, ie the packing department.

Step 2: apportionment of shared overheads to responsibility centres

- Indirect costs that relate to more than one responsibility centre must be shared between these centres using a fair method to apportion the costs.

- For example, heating costs could use comparative floor areas to work out the proportion of the total cost that should be applied to each responsibility centre.

Note that these first two steps may be carried out at the same time, depending on how the information is presented. Step 3 is explained on the next page.

Step 3: re-apportionment of service overheads to responsibility centres

■ The first two steps are likely to result in costs being allocated and apportioned to **service cost centres**. These are responsibility centres that are not involved in the production of finished products but instead provide support to the production responsibility centres.

■ Examples of **service cost centres** are stores and cleaning services. In order for these costs to be shared across the finished products, they must be re-apportioned to the responsibility centres that benefit from their services.

■ An example of data to use to re-apportion stores costs could be the number of issues to each production responsibility centre. If the fabrication department received twice as many issues as the assembly department, it would bear twice as much cost.

Step 4: calculation of budgeted overhead absorption (recovery) rate

■ The previous three steps will have resulted in **all** the indirect production costs being allocated to the responsibility centres that are involved in direct production.

■ These cost totals can then be used to calculate absorption rates. This process is explained in the next chapter.

The extended worked examples that follow show how allocation, apportionment and re-apportionment (Steps 1, 2 and 3) are carried out.

●●●●●●●●●●●●●●●●●●●●●●●●●●●●

EXAMPLE – apportionment of costs – data

A factory has three responsibility centres, with the following data available:

Responsibility Centre	Floor space (Square metres)	Non-current assets (Carrying amount £)	Stores Issues to (Number)
Assembly	800	30,000	7,500
Finishing	400	10,000	2,500
Stores	400	20,000	-
	1,600	60,000	10,000

The **budgeted overheads** for the period are as follows:

		£
Rent		40,000
Indirect labour:	Assembly	25,000
	Finishing	15,000
	Stores	34,000
Depreciation		12,000
Other property overheads		24,000

EXAMPLE – the decisions to be made

- ▓ The first decision is to see which budgeted costs can be allocated and which need to be apportioned:

  - the **indirect labour costs** all relate to specific responsibility centres and can therefore be allocated straightaway

  - **other costs** relate to more than one centre and so must be apportioned

- ▓ Now you need to decide which data is most suitable for apportioning each relevant cost. In this simple example there are limited choices:

  - **rent** normally relates to the size of the building; it therefore makes sense to use the floor space to apportion the cost to the responsibility centres

  - **depreciation** relates to the non-current assets; in the absence of more specific information, the assets' carrying value is the most appropriate data

  - **other property overheads** relate to the building and so floor space seems the most appropriate data to use

We will now show how these decisions are implemented, before going on to examine the re-apportionment of the stores costs, as it is a service cost centre.

EXAMPLE (steps 1 & 2) – the allocation and apportionment calculations

This table below shows how the decisions on the previous page are put into practice:

Overhead	Basis	Total £	Assembly £	Finishing £	Stores £
Rent	Floor space	40,000	20,000	10,000	10,000
Indirect Labour	Allocation	74,000	25,000	15,000	34,000
Depreciation	Carrying amount	12,000	6,000	2,000	4,000
Other Property	Floor space	24,000	12,000	6,000	6,000
Subtotals		150,000	63,000	33,000	54,000

Example: apportionment of rent is calculated as follows:

Total floor space of the factory = 800 + 400 + 400 = 1,600 square metres.

The total rent of £40,000 is apportioned to each responsibility centre using the proportion of this total space that it occupies:

Assembly	£40,000 x (800 ÷ 1,600)	= £20,000
Finishing	£40,000 x (400 ÷ 1,600)	= £10,000
Stores	£40,000 x (400 ÷ 1,600)	= £10,000

Apportionments of the other overhead costs are calculated using the proportions in each responsibility centre of the relevant total (ie carrying amount or floor space).

EXAMPLE (step 3) – the re-apportionment of stores costs

We now need to decide how to **re-apportion** the stores costs and carry out the necessary calculations.

■ Stores is a service cost centre and not directly involved in production.

■ The total cost of stores needs to be re-apportioned, based on the benefit that it provides to the production responsibility centres that it services.

■ The best available data to use for this is the number of **stores issues**.

The starting point of the calculation is the subtotals line from the table on the last page:

	Basis	Total £	Assembly £	Finishing £	Stores £
Subtotals (b/f)		150,000	63,000	33,000	54,000
Re-apportionment of stores total cost	number of issues		40,500	13,500	(54,000)*
Totals		150,000*	103,500	46,500	0

The re-apportionment calculation uses the same approach as before, but this time using the share of the total issues. Assembly (for example) is calculated as:

£54,000 x (7,500 ÷ 10,000) = £40,500.

*Note: total Stores cost is deducted, leaving the amount in the Total column unchanged.

re-apportionment of overheads – some more detail

▦ **direct method**

Re-apportionment can be straightforward, as in the last worked example where the cost of a service cost centre is spread directly over the production centres. This is known as the 'direct method'.

▦ **step-down apportionment**

A more complicated situation can arise when there are several service cost centres, and one (or more) of them may benefit **another service cost centre** as well as production cost centres. In this case you must deal with the re-apportionment of any service cost centres that benefit other service cost centres first. This is known as 'step-down' apportionment.

EXAMPLE – step-down apportionment

There are two service cost centres:
Maintenance benefits only the production centres.
Canteen benefits the maintenance cost centre as well as the production centres.

The order of re-apportionment is:

1 **Canteen** – this will add to **maintenance** and also the other responsibility centres
2 **Maintenance** – the increased total cost is re-apportioned to the production centres

8 Absorption of overheads

CHARGING THE COSTS TO THE PRODUCTS

In the last chapter we showed how budgeted indirect costs are charged to production responsibility centres. This involved steps 1 to 3 shown in the diagram on page 32.

Now we explain the final stage, step 4, in which these costs are used to calculate overhead absorption rates which can be applied to the products.

the budgeted overhead recovery (absorption) rate

- The **recovery rate** is a mechanism for charging some of the total budgeted costs in each production centre to products that are made there.

- The total budgeted costs for a production centre are divided by selected budgeted data (for example, the number of labour hours worked in that centre) to calculate the **budgeted overhead recovery rate**.

  For example, if labour hours had been used, the recovery rate would be expressed in '£ per labour hour'.

main absorption bases

Each budgeted overhead recovery rate uses an **absorption base** that is decided on by examining the relevant production centre and the way in which it operates.

■ **direct labour hours**

This 'base' can be used for production which is labour-intensive. The absorption rate is calculated by dividing the budgeted overheads by the budgeted number of direct labour hours.

Budgeted overhead recovery rate per direct labour hour =

$$\frac{\textit{budgeted overheads for production centre}}{\textit{budgeted direct labour hours for production centre}}$$

■ **machine hours**

This base is useful for machine-intensive operations and where a large part of the overheads relates to the cost of operating machinery.

It is calculated by dividing budgeted overheads by budgeted machine hours.

Budgeted overhead recovery rate per machine hour =

$$\frac{\textit{budgeted overheads for the production centre}}{\textit{budgeted machine hours for the production centre}}$$

■ volume bases

These are often used by service sector organisations. An example is miles travelled by a bus company.

This base is calculated by dividing the budgeted overheads by the budgeted chosen volume – for example, budgeted miles for a bus company:

Budgeted overhead recovery rate per mile travelled =

$$\frac{\textit{budgeted overheads for the bus company}}{\textit{budgeted miles travelled by the bus company}}$$

EXAMPLE (step 4) – using overhead absorption (recovery) rates

This example uses the budgeted costs from the previous worked example (see pages 35-38) and additional information to illustrate the calculation of the most appropriate hourly overhead recovery rates to apply to the two production centres, Assembly and Finishing:

Centre	Total	Budgeted Direct Labour Hours	Budgeted Machine Hours
Assembly	£103,500	3,000	15,000
Finishing	£ 46,500	9,300	0

Assembly is machine-intensive because it has many more budgeted machine hours than budgeted direct labour hours. Therefore **machine hours** is likely to be the most appropriate absorption base. The overhead recovery rate is calculated as:

£103,500 ÷ 15,000 hours = £6.90 per machine hour

Finishing involves only labour, so the appropriate absorption base is **labour hours**. The overhead recovery rate is calculated as:

£46,500 ÷ 9,300 hours = £5.00 per direct labour hour

absorption (recovery) of overheads

When the budgeted information has been used to calculate the budgeted overhead recovery rates, these rates are used to charge (absorb) overheads to products or services.

Because the rates are based on budgeted figures that may not be entirely accurate, discrepancies – under-absorption or over-absorption – may arise by the end of the period.

■ **Under-absorption**

Under-absorption, or under-recovery, arises when the actual overheads for the period are greater than the total absorbed (recovered) into all the products or services. If this occurs, the difference must be debited to the statement of profit or loss as an extra cost. This means that product costs during the period were actually greater than expected.

■ **Over-absorption**

Over-absorption, or over-recovery, is the opposite – more overheads have been absorbed (recovered) into products than the overheads actually cost. This will result in a credit to the statement of profit or loss, as costs have been overstated during the period.

There will always be a small amount of over-absorption or under-absorption. Large amounts mean that the costing data (and maybe the costing system) should be reviewed, as the bugeted unit cost is either too high (over-absorption) or too low (under-absorption).

● ●

EXAMPLE – absorption of overheads

This example uses the data from the previous example to demonstrate how overheads are absorbed by products, and how under-absorption or over-absorption of overheads can occur. The data is as follows:

Budgeted overheads:	Assembly	£103,500
	Finishing	£46,500
Budgeted machine hours:	Assembly	15,000
Budgeted direct labour hours:	Finishing	9,300
Budgeted overhead recovery rate:	Assembly	£6.90 per machine hour
Budgeted overhead recovery rate:	Finishing	£5.00 per direct labour hour

The company makes two products, Product A and Product B:

Product A needs 2 machine hours in Assembly and 1 direct labour hour in Finishing

Product B needs 5 machine hours in Assembly and 4 direct labour hours in Finishing

EXAMPLE (continued) – calculation of overhead cost in each product

During the period the company made 3,000 units of Product A and 1,800 units of Product B.

Product A

In each unit of Product A, overheads will be absorbed:

Assembly overheads: £6.90 x 2 machine hours	=	£13.80
Finishing overheads: £5.00 x 1 direct labour hour	=	£ 5.00
Total overheads absorbed into each unit of Product A		£18.80

Product B

In each unit of Product B, overheads will be absorbed:

Assembly overheads: £6.90 x 5 machine hours	=	£34.50
Finishing overheads: £5.00 x 4 direct labour hours	=	£20.00
Total overheads absorbed into each unit of Product B		£54.50

actual overhead costs incurred

You are now told that during the period the actual overheads incurred were:
Assembly £100,000 and Finishing £53,000.

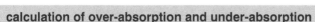

calculation of over-absorption and under-absorption

The calculation of the overheads of each responsibility centre that are absorbed (recovered) into the products made are as follows:

		Assembly	Finishing
		£	£
Product A:			
Assembly:	3,000 x £13.80	41,400	
Finishing:	3,000 x £5.00		15,000
Product B:			
Assembly	1,800 x £34.50	62,100	
Finishing	1,800 x £20.00		36,000
Total overheads absorbed (recovered):		103,500	51,000
Comparison with the actual cost of overheads:		100,000	53,000
Assembly is **over-absorbed**:		3,500	
Finishing is **under-absorbed**:			2,000

Conclusion: under-recovery in Finishing means that not all the actual overheads have been accounted for – the £2,000 must be ultimately debited to the statement of profit or loss. Over-absorption in Assembly means that more costs were recovered than were actually incurred, so £3,500 will be credited to the statement of profit or loss.

9 Cost accounting bookkeeping

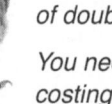

DEBITS AND CREDITS FOR COSTING

Cost accounting bookkeeping follows the same general rules as other areas of double-entry bookkeeping.

You need to make sure that you can apply these rules to account for costing transactions.

areas which involve cost accounting bookkeeping

The main areas that you need to deal with are those already explained in this Guide:

- **accounting for materials** – purchase of inventory and issues from stores to production

- **accounting for labour** – linking the payroll accounting system with the analysis of labour costs

- **accounting for overheads** – absorption (recovery) of overheads and the treatment of under-absorption and over-absorption

accounting for materials

Materials are purchased and entered into the Inventory account; then as they are issued from stores they are transferred to a Production account (usually as a direct cost).

The **journal entries** will be:

Purchase of inventory: **Debit** specific Inventory account
Credit Bank or Payables ledger control account

Transfer to production: **Debit** relevant Production account
Credit specific Inventory account

Note that a variety of names for accounts and/or relevant coding may be used.

EXAMPLE – accounting for materials

A manufacturing company uses the following codes for some of its accounts:

Description	Code
Raw materials – Rubber compound	1200
Raw materials – Plastic pellets	1300
Raw materials – 5mm steel cable	1400
Bank	3000
Payables ledger control	5000
Wages control	6000
Production direct material costs	7100
Production direct labour costs	7200
Production indirect material costs	7300
Production indirect labour costs	7400
Non-production indirect material costs	8300
Non-production indirect labour costs	8400

EXAMPLE – accounting for materials (continued)

The following two transactions took place. The journals that are used to record each transaction are shown below. VAT is ignored.

■ The purchase (on credit) into inventory of 5,000 kilos of plastic pellets at a cost of £5.80 per kilo.

	Code	Debit (£)	Credit (£)
Raw materials – Plastic pellets	1300	29,000	
Payables ledger control	5000		29,000

■ The transfer from inventory into production of 2,500 kilos of rubber compound, valued at £4.00 per kilo. Rubber compound is used directly in production.

	Code	Debit (£)	Credit (£)
Production direct material costs	7100	10,000	
Raw materials – Rubber compound	1200		10,000

accounting for labour

Payroll is normally analysed through a Wages and salaries control account.

The cost of direct and indirect labour can then be transferred to the relevant Production account (direct or indirect) or Non-production account (indirect).

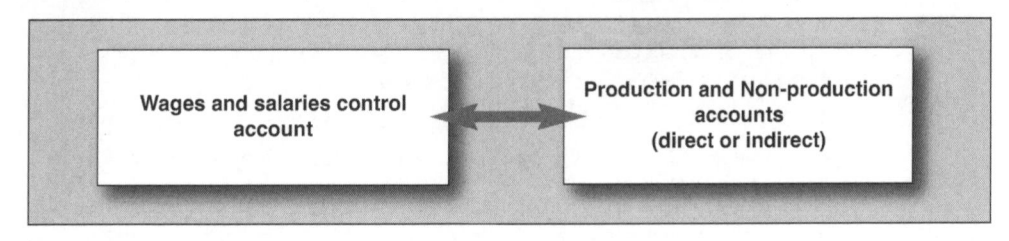

The **journal entries** will be:

Debit	**Direct production account**	(with direct part of labour cost)
Debit	**Production overhead account**	(with relevant indirect part of labour cost)
Debit	**Non-production overhead account**	(with relevant indirect part of labour cost)
Credit	**Wages and salaries control account**	(with total labour costs)

EXAMPLE – accounting for labour

A manufacturing company uses the following codes for its labour cost accounts:

Description	Code
Wages control	6000
Production direct labour costs	7200
Production indirect labour costs	7400
Non-production indirect labour costs	8400

The total **cost of salaries and wages for the month** was £83,860, made up of the following:

Salaries of office managers and staff	£38,560
Wages of production supervisors	£11,200
Wages of production operatives	£34,100

The individual **journal entries** to record these transactions are shown on the next page.

Salaries of office managers and staff

	Code	Debit (£)	Credit (£)
Non-production indirect labour costs	8400	38,560	
Wages and salaries control	6000		38,560

Wages of production supervisors

	Code	Debit (£)	Credit (£)
Production indirect labour costs	7400	11,200	
Wages and salaries control	6000		11,200

Wages of production operatives

	Code	Debit (£)	Credit (£)
Production direct labour costs	7200	34,100	
Wages and salaries control	6000		34,100

accounting for overheads

The actual overhead costs are debited to the relevant Overheads account (or Overheads control account) as they are incurred. The absorbed (recovered) overheads are credited to this account and debited to a Production account. The final balance on the Overheads account will represent the over-recovery or under-recovery of overheads.

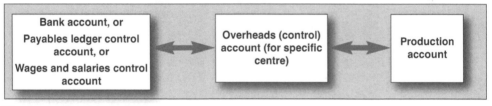

The **journal entries** will be:

Build up of actual costs: **Debit** relevant Overheads account
    Credit Bank / Payables ledger control / Wages and salaries control

Absorption of overheads: **Debit** relevant Production account
    Credit relevant Overheads account

Over- (under-) recovery: **Debit** (or Credit) relevant Overheads account
    Credit (or Debit) statement of profit or loss

EXAMPLE – accounting for overheads

A manufacturing company makes two products – Ayeprod and Beeprod.
The company uses the following codes for some of its cost accounts:

Description	Code
Total cost of Ayeprod production	9000
Total cost of Beeprod production	9200
Production overheads control account	9500
Statement of profit or loss	9900

The month-end balance of the Production overheads control account is £231,560 debit.
This represents the actual total production overheads incurred during the month.

During the month:

- 3,600 units of Ayeprod were produced
- Each unit of Ayeprod absorbs £28 of production overhead
- 5,400 units of Beeprod were produced
- Each unit of Beeprod absorbs £23 of production overhead

The absorption of overheads has not yet been recorded in the cost accounts.

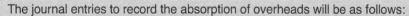

The journal entries to record the absorption of overheads will be as follows:

	Code	Debit (£)	Credit (£)
Total cost of Ayeprod production	9000	100,800	
Production overheads control account	9500		100,800
Total cost of Beeprod production	9200	124,200	
Production overheads control account	9500		124,200

These transactions will result in a debit balance on the Production overheads control account of £6,560 (ie £231,560 – £100,800 – £124,200).

This represents under-recovery of overheads for the month, because the amounts recovered are less than the overheads actually incurred. This balance will be transferred (as an additional cost) to the statement of profit or loss as follows:

	Code	Debit (£)	Credit (£)
Statement of profit or loss	9900	6,560	
Production overheads control account	9500		6,560

10 Specific costing methods

WHY ARE THERE DIFFERENT METHODS?

Costing systems are put in place to help managers to run their organisations.

There are many different methods of costing.

The activities that organisations carry out vary, and so an organisation should choose the method of costing that best meets its needs.

methods of costing

The main types of costing are listed below and explained in full on the next three pages.

- **unit costing** – used where a large number of units of each product are produced
- **job costing** – used where each 'job' undertaken by a business is different
- **batch costing** – used where batches of products are made to different specifications
- **service costing** – used where the organisation provides a service

●●●●●●●●●●●●●●●●●●●●●●●●●●●

■ **unit costing**

- calculates the cost of each individual unit

- is the costing method that has been illustrated so far in this book

- is most suited for organisations that produce several different products and in large quantities

    Examples: a furniture manufacturer, a car component manufacturer

■ **job costing**

- is used where each product or service that is produced is a 'one-off' job

- collects together all the costs for that particular job

- each job will normally have a different cost based on the customer's individual requirements

    Examples: a fitted kitchen, a car repair, a wedding reception

■ **batch costing**

- a variation of unit costing that is used when items are made in batches

- the items in the batch are identical, and the costs calculated for the whole batch

- a batch of a particular product will often be made and then discontinued in order to make way for production of another and different batch

- the cost per unit of a completed batch can be calculated as:

$$\frac{total\ batch\ cost}{the\ number\ of\ units\ in\ the\ batch}$$

Examples: 'new season' fashion clothing, bottles of apple juice, a type of pizza

■ service costing

- – a costing method that is used in service industries

- – useful where there are continuous activities that can be thought of as multiples of a simple measure of output

- – the cost per unit of a service can be calculated as:

$$\frac{total\ cost\ of\ providing\ the\ service}{chosen\ measure\ of\ output}$$

> *Example: 'cost per passenger mile' for a bus company, cost per occupied room night for a hotel, cost per haircut*

11 Unit costing

WHAT IS SO DIFFERENT ABOUT UNIT COSTING?

In its simplest form, unit costing involves collecting all the costs and dividing the total by the total output for the period to get a cost per unit.

But, as we will see in this chapter, unit costing becomes more difficult when work-in-progress and normal and abnormal losses are involved in the calculations.

unit costing – the basics

Unit costing is used for **continuous production,** which means the costs are worked out for a **period of time**.

The total costs for the period are then divided by the number of units for the same period to give a cost per unit of output (cost unit):

$$cost\ per\ unit = \frac{total\ costs\ of\ production\ for\ the\ period}{number\ of\ units\ for\ the\ period}$$

The example which follows shows, step-by-step, how unit costing works.

EXAMPLE – unit costing

The 'FudgeChoc' confectionery bar is produced continually.

During the month of November, 7,300,000 confectionery bars were produced with production costs as follows:

Production costs	£
Materials	840,000
Direct labour	304,000
Production overheads	316,000
Total production cost	1,460,000

Cost per bar of FudgeChoc:

$$\frac{£1,460,000}{7,300,000} = £0.20 \text{ per bar}$$

dealing with work-in-progress

In the FudgeChoc example on the previous page it is assumed that the product is started and finished in the given period.

But this is not always the case and you will have to deal with part-completed items, ie the **work-in-progress** at the end of the given period.

So that you can share out the costs of the process in a fair way you will need to know the **degree of completeness** of these unfinished products so that you can calculate the number of **equivalent units** for costing purposes. The formula for this is:

number of units-in-progress x percentage of completeness = equivalent units

> **Example:**   200 units which are 50% complete, the calculation is:
>
> 200 units x 50% = 100 equivalent units

a further complication – adjusting for materials, labour and overheads

The example above assumes that all the elements of cost – materials, labour and overheads – are all at the same level of completeness, but in reality these three percentages of completion may be different. For example, the materials completion percentage may be 90%, the labour percentage 40% and the overheads percentage 40%.

The method of dealing with this situation is illustrated in the worked example which follows.

EXAMPLE – process costing involving work-in-progress

At the start of January, SupaPulse Ltd, a company that produces lentil crisps for supermarkets, had no work-in-progress following the Christmas break.

At the end of January 564,000 packets of lentil crisps had been produced, and an additional 40,000 packets were still in process as follows:

  90% materials used

  40% direct labour used

  40% overheads used

During January the process incurred the following costs:

Direct materials	£21,000
Direct labour	£46,400
Overheads	£40,600
Total	£108,000

You are to calculate the cost per equivalent unit (packets), and also the total cost of the completed January production and of the work-in-progress (see next page).

Cost per equivalent unit (packet)

This can be worked out using the formula:

total cost ÷ (completed units + equivalent units) = cost per unit

	total cost		equivalent units	workings of cost per equivalent unit		cost per unit (£)
Direct materials	£21,000	÷	600,000	564,000 + (90% x 40,000)	=	0.035
Direct labour	£46,400	÷	580,000	564,000 + (40% x 40,000)	=	0.080
Overheads	£40,600	÷	580,000	564,000 + (40% x 40,000)	=	0.070
						0.185

Cost of completed production:

£0.185 x 564,000 units   =   **£104,340**

Cost of work-in-progress:

Direct materials	£0.035 x (40,000 x 90%)	=	£1,260
Direct labour	£0.080 x (40,000 x 40%)	=	£1,280
Overheads	£0.070 x (40,000 x 40%)	=	£1,120
			£3,660

Note that the cost of completed production of £104,340, plus the cost of closing work-in-progress of £3,660, equals the total costs of the period of £108,000.

The closing work-in-progress will form the opening work-in-progress for the next period.

the Production account

The **Production account** is used to record production costs.

The costs of the inputs to production are debited to the Production account, and the account is subsequently credited when the total costs of the finished goods are transferred to the Finished goods account.

The figures from the worked example on the previous page are used below to illustrate a simple Production account.

Dr	**Production Account**		Cr
	£		£
Inputs	108,000		
		Finished goods	104,340
		Work-in-progress c/d	3,660
	108,000		108,000

Production accounts often also contain additional columns with details of quantities and units costs as we will see later in this chapter.

production losses and gains

Production often results in losses through wastage of material, and this has to be taken into account. The cost of the 'good' output is calculated by deducting the amount of the normal loss caused by wastage and adding back any scrap value income.

Scrap value is the amount of money that can be realised if waste products from the process are sold.

> *Example:*
> *A business that makes oven chips will account for a certain weight of potatoes, but will expect to lose some of that weight when the potatoes are peeled. The peelings may then be sold at **scrap value**.*

The loss in a process can be classified as a **normal loss** or an **abnormal loss**.

- **Normal losses** are those **expected** (planned for) during production.

    The cost of the losses can be offset by income – the **scrap value** – that may be received from the sale of the wastage. This scrap value will be accounted for in the Production account.

> *Example:*
> *The oven chips normal (expected) loss is 10%, so for every 100kg of potatoes input, 10kg will be lost but this may then be offset by the sale of the peelings.*

■ **Abnormal losses** are losses **in excess of any normal losses**. As they are unexpected they are accounted for separately by valuing the abnormal loss at the same unit cost as the expected good output. This abnormal loss will be offset by any scrap value of just the abnormal part of the loss.

Example:
If the oven chips' normal (expected) loss from peeling is 10% for every 100kg of potatoes, but the actual loss is 15%, the abnormal loss will be:

15% actual loss minus 10% normal loss = 5% abnormal (unexpected loss).

We will now illustrate normal and abnormal losses and their accounting treatment in the extended worked example.

EXAMPLE – normal and abnormal losses

A process involves inputting 20,000 kg of material. There are normal losses of 2,000 kg, so the expected good output is 18,000 kg.

The input costs incurred in production during a period are £110,000.

The actual output during the period was 17,500 kg due to abnormal losses of 500 kg.

All the losses (normal and abnormal) are sold for scrap at £1 per kg.

The cost per unit of the expected output is calculated as follows:

(Input costs – scrap value of normal loss) ÷ expected output

(£110,000 – (2,000kg x £1)) ÷ 18,000kg = £6.00 per kg

This is used to value the actual output: 17,500kg x £6.00 = £105,000.

The abnormal loss is initially valued at the same cost per unit as the expected output: 500kg x £6.00 = £3,000.

This is then reduced to £2,500 by deducting the scrap income of £500.

The Process account then appears as follows:

Production Account							
Details	Qty kg	Unit cost £	Total cost £	Details	Qty kg	Unit cost £	Total cost £
Inputs	20,000	5.50	110,000	Normal loss Finished goods Abnormal loss	2,000 17,500 500	1.00 6.00 6.00	2,000 105,000 3,000
	20,000		110,000		20,000		110,000

Note carefully how the figures on the Production account are arrived at:

▓ The normal loss credit entry of £2,000 results from the normal scrap income.

▓ The Abnormal loss account will be:
 − debited with the £3,000 from the Production account, and
 − credited with income of £500 from the additional scrap income

The net debit balance of £2,500 on the Abnormal loss account will be transferred as a debit to the statement of profit or loss.

12 Cost behaviour

HOW DO COSTS BEHAVE?

The topic of cost behaviour examines how costs can change in the short term when the level of output changes.

Remember! These cost categories relate to what happens to the total costs – not the costs per unit.

the categories of cost

There are four main categories of cost:

- **fixed costs** – which remain the same when output changes

- **variable costs** – which vary in line with the level of output

- **stepped fixed costs** – costs which increase in 'steps' as output increases

- **semi-variable costs** – costs which include both fixed costs and also variable costs

These four categories are explained and illustrated with graphs on the next two pages.

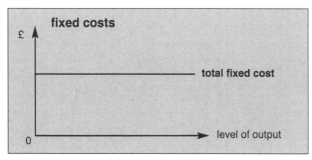

A cost is described as a **fixed cost** if the total cost does not change when the level of output changes.

Example: factory rent

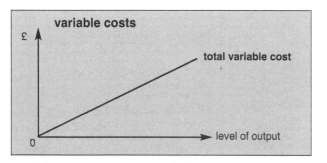

A cost is described as a **variable cost** if the total cost varies in direct proportion to the level of output.

Example: direct material

A cost is described as a **stepped cost** if its total changes in steps at certain levels of output, but remains unchanged in between.

Example: the cost of taking on an extra supervisor when production increases.

A cost is described as a **semi-variable cost** if the total cost is made up of a variable part and a fixed part.

Example: a telephone bill which includes a line rental (fixed) and a unit cost for each call (variable).

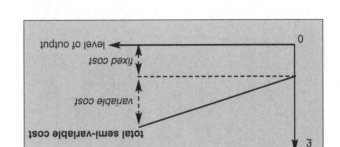

stepped costs

total stepped cost

level of output

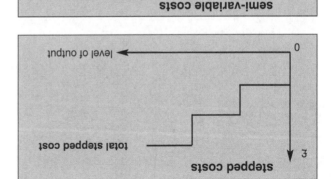

semi-variable costs

total semi-variable cost

variable cost

fixed cost

level of output

analysing semi-variable costs

If we have information about the total semi-variable costs at two different activity levels, we can analyse the costs into the fixed and variable elements using the 'high-low' method. The two activity levels chosen are normally a 'high' one and a 'low' one. This method then allows us to use these figures to predict total costs at other activity levels.

calculation method

1   Calculate the differences between two sets (high and low) of
    – cost totals, and
    – activity levels

2   Divide the cost difference by the activity difference to obtain the **variable cost per unit** of activity.
    Then choose one of the cost totals and use the variable cost per unit to calculate the amount of **variable costs contained within the total costs.**

3   Deduct these **variable costs** from the total cost . . . the result will be the **fixed cost.**

    We now have the fixed cost (in total) and the variable cost (per unit) and these can be used to calculate the total costs at other activity levels. This type of calculation is shown in a worked example on the next page.

EXAMPLE – analysing semi-variable costs

1   You are given the total costs for two different levels of output of units.
    You then calculate the differences between the two sets of figures:

	Units	**Total costs** (£)
	9,900	162,250
minus	6,400	136,000
Differences:	3,500	26,250

You will see from this that it costs £26,250 to produce an additional 3,500 units.

This is all **variable cost**.

2   Using the difference figures you can then calculate the **variable cost per unit**:

£26,250 ÷ 3,500 = £7.50 per unit

Using this figure of £7.50 per unit you can now work out the variable costs
contained in the total cost of producing one of these two output levels.

In this case if you take the higher total, ie 9,900 units, the variable costs will be:

9,900 (units) x £7.50 (variable cost per unit) = £74,250

3 The next step is to work out the **fixed cost** element. We will use the output level of 9,900 units and the formula: *total costs – variable costs = fixed costs*

	£
Total cost of 9,900 units (see step 1 above)	162,250
minus variable costs (9,900 units x £7.50)	74,250
= fixed cost:	88,000

This process then can be used to calculate total costs for other levels of output.

sample further calculation based on the example figures shown above:

We know the variable costs are £7.50 per unit and the fixed costs are £88,000.

The total cost at (say) 8,000 units will therefore be:

	£
Variable costs (£7.50 x 8,000)	60,000
Fixed costs	88,000
Total costs	148,000

13 Marginal and absorption costing

WHAT IS THE DIFFERENCE?

Marginal costing and absorption costing are two different methods of costing, and are used for two different purposes.

Marginal costing is largely based on variable costs rather than on fixed costs and works out the cost of producing one extra unit of output; it is useful for decision making by management.

*Absorption costing incorporates variable costs **and fixed costs** into the cost of producing one unit of output (as explained in Chapter 7).*

key features – marginal costing

- ▨ separates variable costs from fixed costs
- ▨ values products or services only using variable costs
- ▨ treats fixed costs (eg annual rent) as relating to periods of time, not products
- ▨ calculates 'contribution' as revenue less variable costs
- ▨ is especially useful for short-term decision making

key features – absorption costing

- ■ analyses costs by element and nature (direct/indirect)
- ■ absorbs indirect costs into products or services
- ■ uses pre-determined rates and so can be imprecise
- ■ provides a product cost that includes **all** costs of production
- ■ is used in financial statements for inventory valuation

cost analysis and terminology – marginal and absorption costing

The types of cost data used by the two costing methods are shown in this diagram:

marginal costing	absorption costing
variable costs variable direct materials, labour, expenses and overheads	**direct costs** direct materials, labour expenses
fixed costs fixed production overheads	**indirect costs** variable and fixed production overheads

profit statements – using marginal and absorption costing

There are differences in approach and terminology between marginal and absorption costing and so the profit statements using each method of costing also differ.

The worked example set out below highlights these differences.

EXAMPLE – profit statement comparison

- A business manufactures desks with costs as follows:

Direct materials	£18 per desk
Direct labour	£12 per desk
Fixed production overheads	£15 per desk

- Direct costs are all variable.

- The overheads are based on making 1,000 desks in a period with fixed production overheads of £15,000 in that period.

- During the period the business made 1,000 desks and sold them all for £70 each.

- There was no opening or closing inventory.

The profit statements using marginal and absorption costing appear as shown below.

MARGINAL COSTING Profit Statement	£	ABSORPTION COSTING Profit Statement	£
Sales revenue	70,000	Sales revenue	70,000
Less variable costs:		Direct costs:	
Materials	18,000	Materials	18,000
Labour	12,000	Labour	12,000
	30,000		30,000
Contribution	40,000	Indirect costs of production	15,000
Less fixed costs:	15,000	Total production costs	45,000
Profit	25,000	Profit	25,000

in this example . . .

■ the two statements use different layouts and terminology

■ the resulting profits are identical

■ the profits would be different using the two methods of costing if there are changes in inventory levels over the period

inventories and reported profits

The valuation of inventories using marginal costing differs from the valuation of inventory using absorption costing:

■ **marginal costing** – inventory is valued at **variable cost**

■ **absorption costing** – inventory is valued at **absorbed cost**

This means that when there are changes in the levels of inventory during the period (between opening and closing inventory) there will be a difference in the reported profit using each of the two costing methods.

EXAMPLE – marginal and absorption costing: differences in profit levels

Using data from the example on the previous page, any closing inventory would be valued as follows:

■ under **marginal costing**: £18 + £12 = £30 per desk

■ under **absorption costing**: £18 + £12 + £15* = £45 per desk
*overheads of (£15,000 ÷ 1,000 desks) = £15

Suppose that in the period 1,000 desks were made, but only 800 were sold, leaving a closing inventory of 200 desks.

The profit statements would then appear as shown below.

MARGINAL COSTING Profit Statement		ABSORPTION COSTING Profit Statement	
	£		£
Sales revenue (800 x £70)	56,000	Sales revenue (800 x £70)	56,000
Less variable costs:		Direct costs:	
Materials	18,000	Materials	18,000
Labour	12,000	Labour	12,000
	30,000		30,000
Less closing inventory (200 x £30):	6,000	Indirect costs of production	15,000
Variable cost of sales	24,000	Total production costs	45,000
		Less closing inventory (200 x £45)	9,000
Contribution	32,000	Production cost of sales	36,000
Less fixed costs:	15,000		
Profit	17,000	Profit	20,000

Note: in this second example the absorption costing approach has included the fixed (indirect) costs (200 x £15) = £3,000 in inventory and carried these costs into the next period. This amount accounts for the difference in profit between the two methods.

14 Activity based costing

A THIRD METHOD OF COSTING

There are some situations where neither marginal costing nor absorption costing will provide the most useful information. Activity based costing (ABC) is a development of absorption costing that charges overheads to production on the basis of activities.

key features – activity based costing

■ provides a more accurate way of charging overheads to cost units

■ identifies the activities that cause overheads to be incurred

■ identifies appropriate 'cost drivers' for each of these activities

■ charges overheads to cost units based on how activities are used

■ copes well with products that are made in different ways (for example, in different batch sizes)

On the following page are examples of activities and cost drivers.

Activity	Cost driver
Set-up of production equipment	Number of set-ups
Issuing components to production	Number of issues
Quality control inspections	Number of inspections

If we know how much it costs to carry out an activity, and what the cost driver is, we can calculate how much of this overhead to charge to each cost unit.

For example, if it costs £120,000 per year to set up production equipment, and there are 48 set-ups carried out (the cost driver) then each production set up cost is £120,000 / 48 = £2,500.

A product made in small batches of 100 items that requires one set-up per batch will incur a set-up cost of £2,500 / 100 = £25 per unit.

A product made in large batches of 10,000 items that requires one set-up per batch will incur a set-up cost of £2,500 / 10,000 = £0.25 per unit.

Overheads relating to the same activity, such as purchasing materials for production, can be grouped together in a cost pool, then attributed to products using the cost driver.

So the wages of procurement staff, their office expenses, depreciation of their computers, etc, will all be collected before calculating the cost per purchase order for production materials.

15 Budgeting

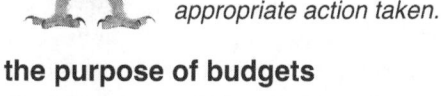

USING BUDGETS

Budgets are financial plans prepared by organisations; they can be fixed, flexible or rolling.

Budgets are prepared in advance and are used to compare actual results against budgeted projections.

Any differences (variances) can then be calculated and analysed and appropriate action taken.

the purpose of budgets

- **decision making** – draft budgets can be prepared based on various possible situations so that the best options can be chosen

- **planning** – budgets enable organisations to plan the resources (eg materials) that will be needed in future periods and identify what outcomes can be expected

- **control** – organisations can compare budgeted and actual results and then take the necessary action where there are differences (variances)

fixed and flexible budgets

Fixed budgets and flexible budgets are two key types of budget you need to know about:

■ **Fixed budgets** are set for the expected level of activity and remain 'fixed' even if the level of activity changes. They are normally used when the budgeted costs are fixed and not dependent on the activity level.
Example: an advertising budget can be set in advance and will not be influenced by production levels.

■ **Flexible (or flexed) budgets** are prepared when the expected income and/or costs will change when activity levels change.
Example: the revenue and costs for operating a restaurant will be very different when the restaurant is nearly empty compared to when it is full of customers.

You need to be able to prepare flexible budgets from an original budget using information about cost behaviour. It is important to remember that you only flex the budget because of different levels of activity – nothing else. Bear in mind that:

– **variable costs** vary in proportion to activity (output)

– **fixed costs** are unchanged (within normal output range)

When a flexible budget has been prepared, it can be compared with the actual results for the same output level, and any variances calculated and investigated.

creating a flexible budget and calculating variances

If you are asked to create a flexible budget and calculate variances, it will normally be because the actual output differs from the budgeted output.

You should create a flexible budget based on the actual activity level (volume) by:

■ recalculating the budgeted income (if any) for the actual volume

■ recalculating each budgeted variable cost for the actual volume

■ leaving unchanged the fixed costs from the original budget

When you have prepared a flexible budget you can then calculate any variances by comparing the flexible budget with the actual figures, remembering that:

■ if actual **revenue** is **higher** than budgeted revenue, the variance is **favourable**

■ if actual **revenue** is **lower** than budgeted revenue, the variance is **adverse**

■ if actual **costs** are **higher** than the budgeted costs, the variances are **adverse**

■ if actual **costs** are **lower** than the budgeted costs, the variances are **favourable**

Note that when a **flexible budget** is adjusted it is also known as a **flexed budget**.

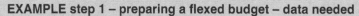

EXAMPLE step 1 – preparing a flexed budget – data needed

In this example, the original budget was based on making and selling 20,000 units.
All budgeted costs except fixed overheads are variable costs.

When the actual figures became available only 18,000 units had been made and sold.

Therefore a flexed budget based on output of 18,000 units is required. The figures
which will form the basis of the flexed budget are as follows:

	Original budget 20,000 units £	Actual figures 18,000 units £
Revenue	300,000	265,000
Less costs:		
Materials	55,000	51,750
Labour	76,000	66,000
Variable overheads	79,000	71,500
Fixed overheads	63,000	61,950
Profit	27,000	13,800

EXAMPLE step 2 – flexing the budget – the calculations

The next step is to flex the budget to the actual volume. The calculation is:

$$\frac{budgeted\ figure\ from\ the\ original\ budget}{number\ of\ units\ from\ original\ budget} \times actual\ number\ of\ units\ produced$$

Note that you must only flex the revenue and costs that change because the volume has changed. The fixed overhead figure of £63,000 is not flexed.

	Original budget	Flexed budget	Actual figures
	20,000 units	18,000 units	18,000 units
	£	£	£
Revenue	300,000	270,000	265,000
Less costs:			
Materials	55,000	49,500	51,750
Labour	76,000	68,400	66,000
Variable overheads	79,000	71,100	71,500
Fixed overheads	63,000	63,000	61,950
Profit	27,000	18,000	13,800

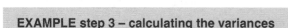

EXAMPLE step 3 – calculating the variances

You now have flexed budget figures and actual figures at the same volume: 18,000 units.

You can now calculate the variances between the actual results and the flexed budget figures.

	Flexed budget 18,000 units	Actual 18,000 units	Variance	
	£	£	£	
Revenue	270,000	265,000	5,000	Adv
Less costs:				
Materials	49,500	51,750	2,250	Adv
Labour	68,400	66,000	2,400	Fav
Variable overheads	71,100	71,500	400	Adv
Fixed overheads	63,000	61,950	1,050	Fav
Profit	18,000	13,800	4,200	Adv

Note: remember to state whether the variance is adverse or favourable.

16 Break-even analysis

THE PURPOSE OF BREAK-EVEN ANALYSIS

Break-even analysis is a quick method of working out the number of units and the sales revenue needed to 'break-even' – ie to make zero profit. Any sales above this point will then make some profit.

Break-even analysis can also be used to work out how to achieve a required level of profit or how far planned sales can fall before the business makes a loss.

calculating break-even

The break-even point can be calculated as:

■ **the number of units**:   = *fixed costs (£) ÷ contribution per unit (£)*

■ **sales value (revenue)**:   = *fixed costs (£) ÷ contribution per £ of sales*

Remember that 'contribution' is the sales revenue less the variable costs.

The **profit-volume ratio** (PV ratio) is *contribution per unit (£) ÷ selling price (£)*.

The profit-volume ratio is also known as the contribution sales (C/S) ratio.

reaching a target profit

The units or revenue (sales value) needed to reach a target profit can be calculated by adding the target profit to the fixed costs before dividing:

■ **number of units**: = *(fixed costs + target profit) ÷ contribution per unit*

■ **revenue**: = *(fixed costs + target profit) ÷ PV ratio*

margin of safety

When the break-even point is known, the **margin of safety** – the difference between expected output and break-even output – can be calculated in units or in revenue:

■ **margin of safety (units)**: = *budgeted sales units – break-even units*

■ **margin of safety (revenue)** = *budgeted sales revenue – break-even revenue*

margin of safety percentage

The margin of safety (units or revenue) can also be expressed as a **percentage**. This shows how far output can fall as a percentage of budgeted unit sales before losses are incurred. The formula is:

(margin of safety (units or revenue) ÷ budgeted units or revenue) x 100

Units or revenue must be used consistently, but will both produce the same percentage.

EXAMPLE – break-even analysis

A company has the following unit data for one of its products.
This data is based on budgeted sales of 20,000 units:

	£
Selling price	50
Variable costs:	
Direct materials	12
Direct labour	13
Overheads	10
Total fixed costs	£240,000

The **break-even point calculations** are as follows:

The contribution per unit:	£50 – (£12 + £13 + £10) = £15
The fixed costs for the period:	£240,000
The profit-volume (PV) ratio:	£15 ÷ £50 = 0.3

Break-even point (in **units**):	£240,000 ÷ £15	= 16,000 units
Break-even point (in **sales revenue**):	£240,000 ÷ 0.3	= £800,000

checking the figures

As the calculation of the break-even point is in both units and revenue it is possible to check that the figures are consistent, ie 16,000 units x £50 = £800,000.

calculating the margin of safety

The margin of safety can be calculated in units, revenue and as a percentage:

- **units:**   20,000 units – 16,000 units   = 4,000 units

- **revenue:**   (20,000 units x £50) – £800,000   = £200,000 revenue

- **percentage:**   (4,000 units ÷ 20,000 units) x 100 = 20%

This means that the budgeted output could fall by 4,000 units (which equals £200,000 revenue) or 20% of budgeted output before losses will be incurred.

calculating a target profit

A target profit set at £90,000 would require sales of:

- **units:**   (£240,000 + £90,000) ÷ £15 = 22,000 units, or

- **revenue:**   (£240,000 + £90,000) ÷ 0.3   = £1,100,000

break-even illustrated on a graph

The break-even graph shown below uses the data and calculations from the worked example, and illustrates the features explained.

A full explanation is set out on the next page.

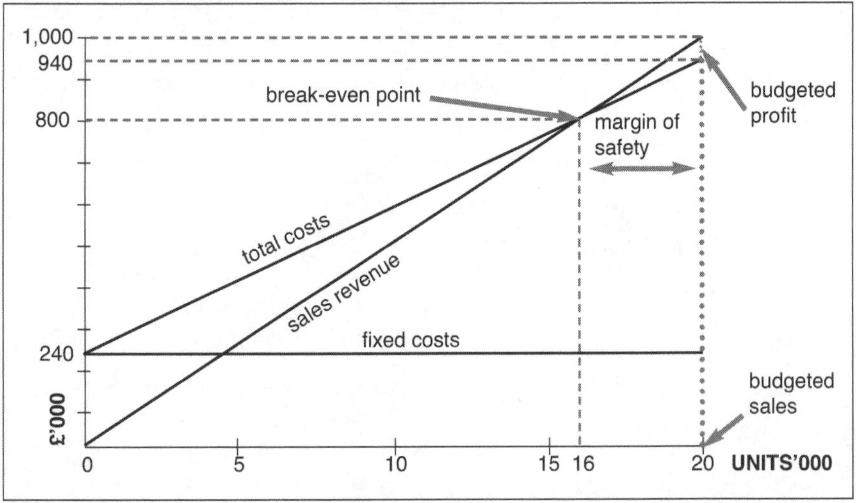

key to the break-even graph

- The **sales revenue line** runs from the zero point (where zero units are sold and revenue is zero) to the budgeted profit where budgeted sales of 20,000 units produces £1,000,000 sales revenue.

- The **fixed cost line** represents costs of £240,000 at all numbers of units.

- The **total cost line** runs from where zero units = £240,000 cost (left-hand axis) to budgeted profit (right-hand side) where 20,000 units = £940,000 total cost.

  This budgeted total cost of £940,000 is made up of £240,000 fixed cost + £700,000 variable cost (ie 20,000 units x £35).

- The **break-even point** is where the sales revenue line crosses the total cost line (ie where sales revenue = total cost). This point is at 16,000 units and £800,000 sales revenue.

- The **budgeted profit** of £60,000 (ie £1,000,000 – £940,000) is shown by the vertical difference between the sales revenue line and the total cost line at 20,000 units.

- The **margin of safety** of 4,000 units (£200,000 sales revenue) is shown by the distance between the break-even point (sales of 16,000 units) and the budgeted figures in units and sales revenue (sales of 20,000 units).

17 Special order pricing

HOW LOW CAN WE GO?

Sometimes extra sales can be generated by selling goods or services to customers who would not buy at the usual prices. The price for special orders can be lower than the normal price, provided it exceeds the marginal cost. In these circumstances 'any contribution is better than no contribution'.

It is important that lowering the price to obtain additional sales does not reduce the demand for goods at the normal prices. Sometimes the special price order may come from a market that the business does not normally sell to – for example overseas.

Lowering prices for some customers is also common in the hotel business where cheap late booking prices avoid leaving rooms empty. Provided these cheap prices exceed the marginal (variable) costs, and do not reduce the level of sales at normal prices, then the strategy will be worthwhile.

EXAMPLE

A company manufactures the 'Titan' product, with unit costs as follows:

	£
Direct materials	12
Direct labour	15
Fixed production overheads	23
Total absorption cost	50

The normal selling price is £70 per unit, and UK sales of 5,000 units are made per year at this price. The company has capacity to make and sell 6,000 units.

It has been ascertained that direct costs behave as variable costs.

A new overseas customer has offered to buy either 200 units per year for £45 each, or 800 units per year for £35 each.

The additional contribution would be either:

200 units x (£45 − (£12 + £15)) = £3,600, or

800 units x (£35 − (£12 + £15)) = £6,400

The order for 800 units at £35 would therefore increase profit by the greatest amount (£6,400) and should therefore be accepted.

18 The importance of cash

CASH IS KING......!

A business can be generating profits but have little cash in the bank or even have an overdraft. Cash is the 'life blood' of a business, so it must ensure it has enough cash to operate.

differences between cash and profit

Cash is the money in an organisation's bank account whilst profit is calculated as income less expenses, allowing for adjustments for accruals, prepayments and non-cash items. The reasons for a low bank balance when an organisation is generating high profits include:

- **purchases of non-current assets** – this will reduce cash balances; profits will only be reduced by the annual depreciation charge on the non-current asset

- **increase in trade receivables** – when goods are sold, profits and trade receivables increase; cash will not increase as customers have not yet paid

- **increase in inventory** – the cash balance reduces as it is used to purchase inventory; profits will increase when the inventory is sold

- ■ **decrease in trade payables** – profit is unaffected by a decrease in trade payables; the cash balance will reduce as suppliers will have been paid
- ■ **prepayment of expenses** – the expenses paid in advance will reduce the cash balance in the year but reduce profit in the next year
- ■ **loan repayments** – cash reduces when the payment is made; profit is not affected
- ■ **drawings** – paying drawings reduces cash at the bank, but there is no effect on profit

Cash may flow into a business when profits reduce or remain unaffected if the opposite situation occurs. For example, a decrease in trade receivables indicates customers are paying, increasing the cash balance, with no effect on profit.

19 Layout of a cash budget

A SUITABLE LAYOUT

The cash budget needs to provide information in a simple format, to show how cash balances are likely to change. It could be produced on a yearly, monthly or even weekly basis, and the same layout is used.

key features of the cash budget

- ■ **Receipts** – shows each type of receipt separately – capital introduced, cash from cash sales and trade receivables, proceeds from disposals of non-current assets
- ■ **Payments** – shows each type of payment separately – purchases of non-current assets, purchases of inventory, payment of trade payables, operating expenses, drawings
- ■ **Summary of the cash position** – shows the net cash flow (**receipts – payments**), opening bank balance at the start of the period and the closing bank balance at the end (**opening bank balance + net cash flow = closing bank balance**)

EXAMPLE OF A CASH FLOW

Joe and Ben Nightingale trading as 'Pet Supplies' Cash budget for four months ending 30 June 20-3				
Receipts	**Jan, £**	**Feb, £**	**Mar, £**	**April, £**
Capital introduced	18,000			
Cash sales	-	600	1,400	2,500
Trade receivables	-	1,200	4,000	6,000
Total receipts for month	**18,000**	**1,800**	**5,400**	**8,500**
Payments				
Non-current assets	7,000			
Purchases	4,000	4,500	5,000	5,000
Other operating expenses	1,300	1,300	1,300	1,300
Drawings	1,200	1,200	1,200	1,200
Total payments for the month	**13,500**	**7,000**	**7,500**	**7,500**
Net cash flow	4,500	(5,200)	(2,100)	1,000
Opening bank balance / (overdraft)	-	4,500	(700)	(2,800)
Closing bank balance / (overdraft)	**4,500**	**(700)**	**(2,800)**	**(1,800)**

Note: February's opening bank balance = January's closing bank balance and so on

20 Forecasting receipts and payments

TIMING OF CASH FLOWS

The cash flow budget needs to allow for the timing differences between invoicing a customer and when they pay. Suppliers invoice the business for purchases and payment is often made one or two months later. This 'lagging' effect must be adjusted for when calculating receipts from credit sales and payments for credit purchases.

receipts from trade receivables

- the business must include cash receipts from trade receivables when it expects them to be received; this could be different to the credit terms given

- prompt payment discounts (PPD) reduce the cash received from credit sales made in the month

- irrecoverable debts will never be received and must be deducted from the cash flow receipts

worked example

Calculate receipts from trade receivables for July to September (ignore VAT)

■ Trade receivables at 1 July are £21,000; credit sales are budgeted to be £45,000 in July, £60,000 in August and £70,000 in September

■ 50% of sales are paid for in the month of sale, with a PPD of 2%

■ 50% of sales pay the month after sales, with no PPD and 3% of these will not pay and should be regarded as irrecoverable

Solution

Receipts from trade receivables			
Month of sale	**July, £**	**August, £**	**September, £**
June sales	21,000		
July sales	22,500	22,500	
August sales		30,000	30,000
September sales			35,000
PPD (2%)	(450)	(600)	(700)
Irrecoverable debt (3%)	(630)	(675)	(900)
Receipts for month	**42,420**	**51,225**	**63,400**

payments to trade payables

■ the business must include cash payments to trade payables when it expects to pay them; this could be different to the credit terms given by suppliers

Note: delaying paying a supplier may result in it refusing to send further goods until the full account is settled, which could delay production.

■ prompt payment discounts (PPD) reduce the cash paid to a supplier for purchases made in the month

worked example

Calculate payments to trade payables for July to September (ignore VAT).

■ Trade payables at 1 July are £18,000; credit purchases are budgeted to be £30,000 in July, £40,000 in August and £45,000 in September

■ 50% of trade payables are paid in the month of purchase, with prompt payment discount (PPD) of 3%

■ 50% of trade payables are paid in the month after purchase, with no PPD

Solution

Payments to trade payables			
Month of purchase	July, £	August, £	September, £
June purchases	18,000		
July purchases	15,000	15,000	
August purchases		20,000	20,000
September purchases			22,500
PPD (3%)	(450)	(600)	(675)
Payments for month	32,550	34,400	41,825

forecasting other receipts and payments

- ▦ other receipts must be included in the cash budget in the month when they are expected to be received (a new loan, additional capital)

- ▦ other payments must be included in the cash budget in the month when they are expected to be paid (wages, operating expenses, loan repayments)

21 Funding purchases of non-current assets

TYPES OF FUNDING

Purchasing non-current assets often requires a large amount of money. The type of funding used depends on the organisation's circumstances. It may choose to fund by: cash, part-exchange or borrowing – loans or hire purchase.

cash purchase

- ■ suitable when the business has enough cash to buy the non-current asset outright and still pay its bills easily

- ■ a purchase on standard 30 days terms is a 'cash' purchase

part exchange

- ■ an old non-current asset is 'traded in' as part of the purchase of a new non-current asset, with the balance being paid by cash or borrowing, often used for new cars or vans

borrowing – loans

- a **loan agreement** with the bank or a finance company (**lender**) for the amount required to purchase the non-current asset
- the organisation will own the non-current asset once it is purchased
- security may be required by the lender
- agreed loan repayments are made to cover the cost and interest
- interest on the loan may be at a fixed or variable rate
- loans can be for 3 – 25 years, often matching to the asset's useful life

borrowing – hire purchase

- a **hire purchase agreement** is made with a finance company
- the organisation will pay a deposit, then can use the non-current asset; the finance company continues to own it
- regular payments are made to the finance company, covering the cost plus interest charges
- the organisation owns the asset once all the payments are made
- typically for 3 – 5 years

Note: overdrafts are short-term finance, so not used for buying non-current assets.

22 Use of resources ratios

THE USE OF RATIOS

Ratios inform owners and managers about the efficiency of the business. They assist in controlling the inventories, trade receivables and trade payables.

Ratios are formulas that produce a number of days, which can be used to measure how efficient the organisation is being with its resources.

How are they used?

- to monitor how much cash is tied up in current assets

- to determine if the organisation is controlling the day-to-day operations effectively

- to consider if cash is being tied up in current assets unnecessarily

- to compare to other similar businesses, to improve operations

What are they and what do they measure?

■ **Inventory holding period (days)**

The number of days inventories are held on average. This depends on the type of goods sold by the business. A bakery may hold only a few days' inventory; a manufacturing business may hold inventory for 60 or 90 days.

■ **Trade receivables collection period (days)**

How many days, on average, trade receivables take to pay the business. This should be in line with the business's credit terms. Comparing this to previous years indicates if credit control is more or less efficient.

■ **Trade payables payment period (days)**

How many days, on average, the business takes to pay suppliers. This should be in line with suppliers' credit terms – taking much longer to pay could adversely affect relationships with suppliers.

■ **Working capital cycle (days)**

The time between paying for inventory and collecting the cash from the customer. The shorter this is, the less working capital is required.

formulas

- **Inventory holding period (days)**

  Formula: Inventories / Cost of sales x 365

- **Trade receivables collection period (days)**

  Formula: Trade receivables / Revenue x 365

- **Trade payables payment period (days)**

  Formula: Trade payables / Cost of sales x 100

- **Working capital cycle (days)**

  Formula: Inventory holding period (days) + Trade receivables collection period (days) – trade payables payment period (days)

the importance of liquidity

▓ insufficient liquidity (i.e. lack of cash to pay short-term debts) can make it difficult for a business to continue to trade

▓ liquidity varies from business to business

how to improve liquidity

▓ obtain additional capital from the owners

▓ raise additional debt finance – loans, hire purchase, overdrafts

how to reduce the working capital cycle to improve cash flow

▓ improve debt collection practices to reduce trade receivables; offer a prompt payment discount (which will reduce profitability)

▓ slow down paying suppliers (without affecting this working relationship) or renegotiate longer terms with suppliers

▓ reduce inventory to lower inventory days, whilst ensuring there is enough to meet customer demand

23 Spreadsheet skills – introduction

THE USE OF SPREADSHEETS

Spreadsheets are an invaluable tool when producing management accounting information. The type of information differs from business to business but will need to be produced and presented in a way that enables managers to understand, plan and control the business.

Text, border and number formatting – What is it used for?

■ Highlights key numbers and information

■ Makes it easy to see the value or currency of numbers within the accounts

■ Clear layout increases the understanding of non-financial managers

Text, border and number formatting – How do you do it?

Use the **Font box (for text)** and **Number box** on the toolbar. Choose the font type and number formats using the dropdown menus, indicated by arrows.

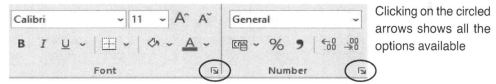

Clicking on the circled arrows shows all the options available

Font buttons: change size or style: **Bold**, *Italic* or <u>underline</u>, add borders or colour.

Number buttons: includes accounting format (£0,000), no. of decimal places or %.

What does it look like?

Statement of Profit or Loss		
Year ended 31 March 20-2		£
Revenue		1,250,600
Total cost		(1,011,585)
Profit		**239,015**
Profit %		*19.11%*

24 Simple formulas and the sum function

THE USE OF FORMULAS AND FUNCTIONS

*Just as you might use a calculator to add up expenses and income, so you can use a formula in a spreadsheet to do the same. Some formulas can be complex and you may also choose to use functions. Let's start by looking at creating straightforward formulas and looking at the **sum** function.*

What are simple formulas and the sum function used for?

■ Adding (+), subtracting (-), dividing (/) or multiplying (*) numbers within cells or typed in, to produce accounting information

■ Use the **sum** function to add up a large column or row of cells containing numbers

Simple formulas and the sum function – How do you do it?

Simple formula: click on a cell and type in the formula, starting with an equals sign '=', choosing the cells to include, and using the correct spreadsheet symbols.

Sum function: use the **Autosum** function (Editing box of the Toolbar) and highlight the cells to add up.

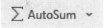

What does it look like?

	A	B
1	**Statement of Profit or Loss**	
2	**Year ended 31 March 20-2**	**£**
3	Revenue	1,250,600
4	Prime cost	(524,700)
5	Production overheads	(126,785)
6	Production cost	(651,485)
7	Overhead costs	(347,300)
8	Finance costs	(12,800)
9	Total cost	(1,011,585)
10	**Profit**	**239,015**
11	*Profit %*	*19.11%*

Sum function and simple formulas:

Cell B9, Total cost is:
=SUM(B6:B8)

Cell B10, Profit is:
=B3+B9

Cell B11, Profit margin % is:
=B10/B3

(Note: costs are negative, as shown by the brackets.)

25 Using simple IF statements

WHY USE AN IF STATEMENT?

*Often accounting information is used to make a decision. An **IF statement** is a good tool to use to do this, particularly as any changes in the costs or income relating to the decision will automatically be accounted for in the IF statement.*

What are simple IF statements used for?

- Determining whether sales staff will be paid a bonus if sales are above a certain amount

- Deciding whether or not to make a new product, based on a required profit

- Deciding whether cost or net realisable value (NRV) is lower, so should be used to value inventory

Simple IF statement – How do you do it?

Let's use an example to help us. We want to automatically insert the lower of cost or NRV.

	A	B	C	D	E	F
1	Inventory valuation					
2				Cost	NRV	IAS 2 value of item
3	Dreamy	Single	32	£ 246.50	£ 199.00	
4	Cosy	Single	13	£ 226.50	£ 299.00	
5	Dreamy City	Single	55	£ 226.50	£ 279.00	
6	Sleepy	Single	13	£ 209.00	£ 199.00	

We want to find the value to use for each inventory item in column F.

Simple IF statement – How do you do it? Cont'd

Click into the cell you are completing – in this case F3.

Use the Insert Function option on the Formulas ribbon, choosing the **IF function**.

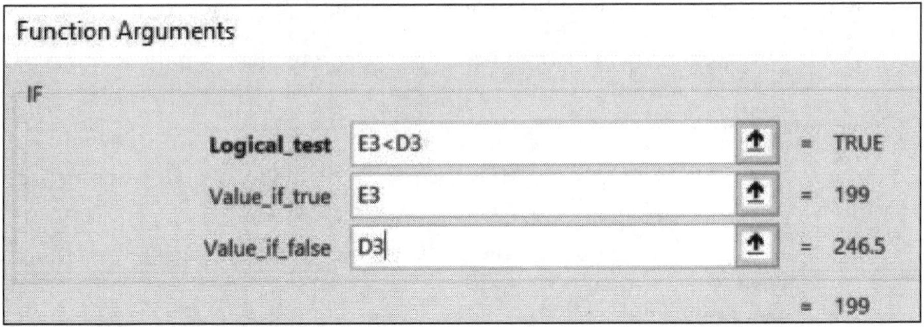

Function Arguments				
IF				
Logical_test	E3<D3	⬆	=	TRUE
Value_if_true	E3	⬆	=	199
Value_if_false	D3	⬆	=	246.5
			=	199

Logical test: We want to know if NRV in column E is lower (<) than Cost in column D.

Value_if_true: If NRV (E3) is lower than Cost (D3), then NRV (E3) is used for the IAS 2 value for the item in F3.

Value_if_false: If the NRV (E3) is NOT lower than cost (D3), then the Cost value (D3) is the IAS 2 value for the item in F3.

Simple IF statement – What does it look like?

	A	B	C	D	E	F
1	**Inventory valuation**					
2				Cost	NRV	IAS 2 value of item
3	Dreamy	Single	32	£ 246.50	£ 199.00	£ 199.00
4	Cosy	Single	13	£ 226.50	£ 299.00	£ 226.50
5	Dreamy City	Single	55	£ 226.50	£ 279.00	£ 226.50
6	Sleepy	Single	13	£ 209.00	£ 199.00	£ 199.00

The highlighted boxes show the lowest value for each inventory item, which the **IF statement** is calculating to go into column F.

Any changes in the values in columns D or E will automatically update column F.

26 Complex IF statements – nested AND/OR

LOGIC CAN BE COMPLICATED

*An **IF statement** can also be combined (nested) with AND and OR, so that more complicated conditions can be met in a situation.*

*Once you have mastered the **IF statement**, including AND or OR is relatively straightforward.*

What are complex IF statements (nested AND/OR) used for?

These types of function could be used when:

- ▓ A salesperson may need to meet two criteria to earn a bonus

- ▓ Discounts may be offered when sales volumes reach a certain amount

- ▓ Agreeing to pay a staff bonus when one or another condition is met

IF statement – nested AND – How do you do it?

Let's look at some sales made by sales staff in the month. The following sales have been made by the four sales staff.

	A	B	C	D	E	F
1	W/c 03/06/20-8					
2	Salesperson	Garden sets	Accessories	Extended warranty	Total	Bonus payable
3	John	£9,465	£1,100	£450	£11,015	
4	Priya	£14,875	£300	£450	£15,625	
5	Cheni	£7,846	£500	£300	£8,646	
6	Tonya	£9,860	£750	£450	£11,060	
7		£42,046	£2,650	£1,650	£46,346	
8	Target per person	£9,500	£600	£400		

A bonus is payable if the salesperson exceeds an overall target of £10,500 and sells above target on accessories. We want to create an **IF statement** including **AND** to show if a bonus is payable in column F for each employee.

IF statement – nested AND – How do you do it? Cont'd

Click into the cell you are completing – in this case F3.

Use the Insert Function option on the Formulas ribbon, choosing the **IF function** again.

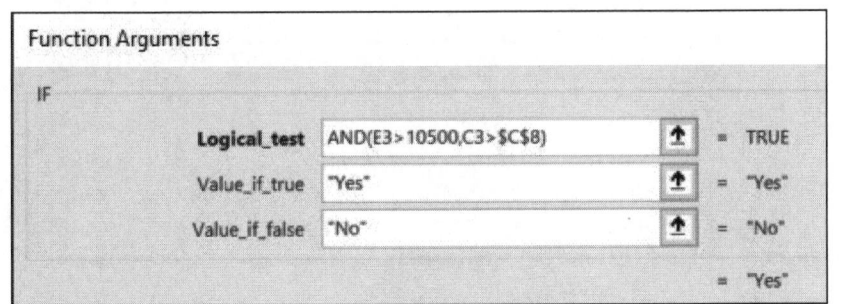

Function Arguments				
IF				
Logical_test	AND(E3>10500,C3>$C$8)	⬆	=	TRUE
Value_if_true	"Yes"	⬆	=	"Yes"
Value_if_false	"No"	⬆	=	"No"
			=	"Yes"

Logical test: The first word 'AND' identifies that we need two conditions met – sales of £10,500 and accessories (C3) to be bigger than the targeted amount ($C$8). Note this is set, using absolute referencing ($), so the formula can be copied down.

Value_if_true: 'Yes', to indicate the bonus is payable. This cell could even include a calculation of the bonus payment.

Value_if_false: 'No' to indicate the bonus is not payable.

IF statement – nested AND – What does it look like?

The formulas for the sales bonuses look like this, and the answers given by the formulas are shown beside them.

Formulas

	A	F
1	W/c 03/06/20-8	
2	Salesperson	Bonus payable
3	John	=IF(AND(E3>10500,C3>$C$8),"Yes","No")
4	Priya	=IF(AND(E4>10500,C4>$C$8),"Yes","No")
5	Cheni	=IF(AND(E5>10500,C5>$C$8),"Yes","No")
6	Tonya	=IF(AND(E6>10500,C6>$C$8),"Yes","No")

Answers

F
Bonus payable
Yes
Yes
No
Yes

As you can see, not all staff get a bonus! Go back and look at page 123 to work through the figures, if you wish, to confirm your understanding.

IF statement – nested OR – How do you do it?

Let's set the bonus now to be earned only if accessories or extended warranties are over target. Using the Insert Function again, let's looks at how this would appear in the Function Wizard for F3:

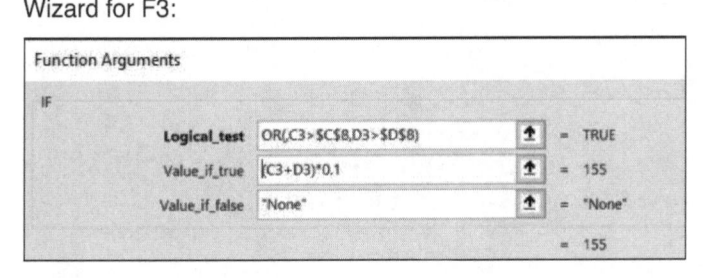

Function Arguments				
IF				
Logical_test	OR(C3>$C$8,D3>$D$8)	↑	=	TRUE
Value_if_true	(C3+D3)*0.1	↑	=	155
Value_if_false	"None"	↑	=	"None"
			=	155

Logical test: The first word 'OR' identifies that we need one of two conditions to be met – either accessories (C3) need to be bigger than target ($C$8) or extended warranties (D3) need to be bigger than the targeted amount ($D$8). Note using absolute referencing ($), means the formula can be copied down.

Value_if_true: This cell contains the calculation of the bonus payment – 10% of the total of accessories (C3) and extended warranty sales (D3).

Value_if_false: 'None' to indicate the bonus is not payable.

IF statement – nested OR – What does it look like?

The formulas for the sales bonuses look like this, and the answers given by the formulas are shown beside them.

Formulas

Answers

	A	F		F
1	W/c 03/06/20-8			
2	Salesperson	Bonus payable		Bonus payable
3	John	=IF(AND(E3>10500,C3>$C$8),"Yes","No")		Yes
4	Priya	=IF(AND(E4>10500,C4>$C$8),"Yes","No")		Yes
5	Cheni	=IF(AND(E5>10500,C5>$C$8),"Yes","No")		No
6	Tonya	=IF(AND(E6>10500,C6>$C$8),"Yes","No")		Yes

The bonus calculation shows when either accessories **OR** the extended warranty target is met, 10% of the total of both is payable.

27 Statistical functions – count, counta, countif

ACCOUNTANTS NEED TO COUNT!

*Sometimes you might need to determine the number of cells with information in them, or the number of blank cells in a set of data. You may even want to find the number of cells containing a particular value or text. This is when the **count** function, along with **counta** and **countif**, can be useful.*

What are the count functions used for?

These functions will give a number as an answer in the following circumstances.

- **count**: counts the number of cells in a range that contain numbers

- **counta**: counts how many cells in a range are not empty

- **countif**: counts the number of cells in a range that contain a particular text or number

Count functions – How do you do them?

Click into the cell you are completing and use the Insert Function option on the Formulas ribbon, choosing the **count**, **counta** or **countif** function.

In this instance, we have selected **counta**:

Function Arguments

Highlight the range of cells in which you want to identify how many are not empty, or enter them individually, a value at a time (up to 255 cells can be entered).

Count functions – What do they look like?

Let's look at an example of employees who make clothing.

	A	B	C
1	**Wednesday 26 May**		
2	**Ali Ghalid**	**Charlotte Holmes**	**Jamal Khalid**
3	**9**	**8**	**7**
4	T-shirt	T-shirt	T-shirt
5	Sweatshirt	Sweatshirt	Shirt
6	Shirt	Shirt	Shirt
7	T-shirt	T-shirt	Sweatshirt
8	Sweatshirt	T-shirt	Shirt
9	Shirt	Sweatshirt	Sweatshirt
10	T-shirt	Sweatshirt	Shirt
11	T-shirt	Shirt	
12	Shirt		

Three employees make clothing and we want to know:

- Whether the employee has completed the amount they have made in row 3 (**count**).

- How many items are made in total (**counta**)?

- How many of each type have been made (**countif**)?

The functions and the answers are shown below, along with the formulas:

	D	E	F
1			
2	**Function**	**Answer**	**Type**
3			
4	COUNT	3	
5	COUNTA	24	
6	COUNTIF	8	T-shirt
7	COUNTIF	7	Sweatshirt
8	COUNTIF	9	Shirt
9			

E
Answer
=COUNT(A3:C12)
=COUNTA(A4:C12)
=COUNTIF(A4:C12,"T-shirt")
=COUNTIF(A4:C12,"Sweatshirt")
=COUNTIF(A4:C12,"Shirt")

28 Statistical functions – Average, Max, Min

INVENTORY ANALYSIS AND MORE...

When you are looking at a large volume of data – for example, inventory lines or employee costs – it can be useful to find an average value, as well as the maximum or minimum amount. Using statistical functions such as **average**, **max(imum)** *and* **min(imum)** *will mean you can do this quickly and accurately.*

What are these functions used for?

These functions can only be used on cells containing numbers and help to find the following in large amounts of data:

- **average**: the average value (total value / number of items in the data)

  e.g. the average value of inventory held or average pay per employee

- **max**: the highest value in the data e.g. the highest paid employee in a week

- **min**: the lowest value in the data e.g. the lowest paid employee in a week

Average, Max & Min – How do you do them?

Click into the cell you are completing and use the Insert Function option on the Formulas ribbon, choosing the *average*, *max* or *min* function.

In this instance, we have selected **average**, using the employee pay information on the following page:

Function Arguments

AVERAGE		
Number1	B3:B9	↥
Number2		↥

Highlight the range of cells you want the average of, or enter them individually, completing Number1, Number2, etc (up to 255 cells can be entered).

Average, Max and Min – What do they look like?

Let's look at some information for weekly paid employees, who make clothing.

	A	B
1	**W/c 25/04/20-9**	
2	**Employee Name**	**Gross Pay**
3	Karen Parsons	£725.00
4	Phil Morris	£594.00
5	Cam Long	£315.00
6	Mariyah Sadiq	£250.00
7	Mo Gee	£474.00
8	Ben Williams	£356.00
9	Anish Bhatt	£421.00
10		£3,135.00
11		

We would like to know:

- The average cost per employee for the week (**average**)
- The highest amount paid to an employee (**max**)
- The lowest amount paid to an employee (**min**)

The functions and the answers are shown below, along with the formulas.

Compare the answer to the data above and you will find the average pay is £447.86 (£3,135.00 divided by 7 staff), Karen Parsons is paid the most, and Mariyah Sadiq the least.

	D	E
1		
2	**Function**	**Answer**
3		
4	AVERAGE	£447.86
5	MAX	£725.00
6	MIN	£250.00
7		

	D	E
1		
2	**Function**	**Answer**
3		
4	AVERAGE	=AVERAGE(B3:B9)
5	MAX	=MAX(B3:B9)
6	MIN	=MIN(B3:B9)
7		

29 Using subtotal

SUBTOTALLING MADE EASY

*Adding subtotals to reports can be a laborious and time-consuming business. Using the **subtotal** function will automate this, making it accurate and fast to do, with a bit of thought.*

*This function can be used to either add up (**subtotal**) or you can use it to find the average, maximum value or minimum value in a set of data, as we did in the previous chapter.*

What is subtotal used for?

Examples include:

- ▓ Subtotalling particular inventory ranges in an inventory report

- ▓ Totalling direct materials, labour or overhead costs ready to summarise for break-even analysis

- ▓ Subtotalling production overheads ready to apportion for overhead rates

Subtotal – How do you do it?

Highlight your data, including the headings row. We are going to look at an example on the next two pages and will use it to illustrate how to use **subtotal** here.

On the **Data** ribbon on the toolbar, in the **Outline** box, choose **Subtotal** and see:

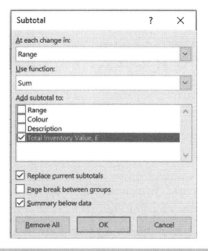

Key points:

At each change in:

Allows you to choose the column of data you want a subtotal for.

Use function:

Choose if you want to total (Sum), Average (Average), find the maximum (Max) or minimum (Min) in each section.

Add subtotal to:

Which column do you want totalled, averaged, etc

NB: Data must be sorted by Range first – see Chapter 31 Manipulating Data.

Subtotal – What does it look like?

We would like to total the inventory value for each range – Dreamy and Cosy. Let's use the subtotal function completed on the previous page on the following data:

	A	B	C	D
1	Range	Colour	Description	Total Inventory Value, £
2	Dreamy	Midnight	Single	6,368.00
3	Dreamy	Midnight	Double	11,571.00
4	Dreamy	Midnight	King Size	5,490.00
5	Dreamy	Midnight	Queen Size	7,293.00
6	Dreamy	Midnight	Super King Size	5,990.00
7	Cosy	Oatmeal	Single	3,464.50
8	Cosy	Oatmeal	Double	11,887.50
9	Cosy	Oatmeal	King Size	7,147.20
10	Cosy	Oatmeal	Queen Size	5,826.00
11	Cosy	Oatmeal	Super King Size	17,387.50

The subtotals are adding up the Dreamy and Cosy Range in the Total Inventory Value column.

1 2 3		A	B	C	D
	1	Range	Colour	Description	Total Inventory Value, £
	2	Dreamy	Midnight	Single	6,368.00
	3	Dreamy	Midnight	Double	11,571.00
	4	Dreamy	Midnight	King Size	5,490.00
	5	Dreamy	Midnight	Queen Size	7,293.00
	6	Dreamy	Midnight	Super King Size	5,990.00
−	7	**Dreamy Total**			36,712.00
	8	Cosy	Oatmeal	Single	3,464.50
	9	Cosy	Oatmeal	Double	11,887.50
	10	Cosy	Oatmeal	King Size	7,147.20
	11	Cosy	Oatmeal	Queen Size	5,826.00
	12	Cosy	Oatmeal	Super King Size	17,387.50
−	13	**Cosy Total**			45,712.70
−	14	**Grand Total**			82,424.70

Clicking on the numbered boxes in the top left-hand corner − 1,2 and 3 − shows the level of detail:

1: Grand Total only

2: Dreamy Total, Cosy Total and Grand Total only

3: All inventory lines, with subtotals

30 Lookup functions

REFERRING TO SET INFORMATION

*Sometimes we might have wage rates or prices on one worksheet that we want to use to calculate job costs on another worksheet. As long as we have a shared reference on each worksheet, such as an employee name or product code, we can use the **lookup** functions: **vlookup** and **hlookup**. This will help ensure the information produced is accurate.*

What are vlookup and hlookup used for?

We could use **vlookup** and **hlookup** for the following:

- Pricing products when invoicing customers

- Apportioning overheads for overhead absorption rates

- Calculating the gross pay of employees with different pay rates

- Costing products using different materials

Lookup – How do you do it?

Look at the reference data – the price list, the wages rates, the material costs – and if they are set out in rows, reading down the page, ie **vertically** presented, use **vlookup**. If the data is set out in columns, reading across the page, **horizontally**, you will need to use **hlookup**.

We are going to work through **vlookup** to find the wages rate per hour for some employees to complete the 'Gross Pay Calculation' in the worksheet below:

⬕	A	B	C	D
1	W/c 02/05/20-9			
2	Employee Name	Hrs	Rate/ hr, £	Gross Pay, £
3	Karen Parsons	39		
4	Phil Morris	40		
5	Cam Long	25		
6	Mariyah Sadiq	31		
7	Mo Gee	24		
8	Ben Williams	10		
9	Anish Bhatt	8		

Lookup – How do you do it? Cont'd

There is a separate table on a different worksheet 'Wages Rates', containing the wage rate for each employee.

We are going to work through **vlookup** to find the wages rates for the employees, as the wage rates table, on the worksheet 'Wage Rates', looks like this:

	A	B
1	**Employee Name**	**Rate/ hr**
2	Karen Parsons	17.00
3	Phil Morris	15.50
4	Cam Long	14.50
5	Mariyah Sadiq	14.50
6	Mo Gee	14.50
7	Ben Williams	14.50
8	Anish Bhatt	14.50

Table is laid out **vertically**, reading from top to bottom, so use **vlookup**

In the cell you want the information in, use the Insert Function choosing **vlookup**.

To find Karen Parson's wage rate in the 'Gross Pay Calculation' worksheet, enter the **vlookup** function in cell C3:

VLOOKUP	
Lookup_value	A3
Table_array	'Wage Rates'!$A$2:$B$8
Col_index_num	2
Range_lookup	FALSE

Lookup value: this is the employee's name, i.e. the reference

Table array: the table you are looking at – in this case cells A2 to B8 in the 'Wage Rates' worksheet

Col_index_num: the column of your Table array where the data you want is located – in the 'Wage Rates' worksheet this is column 2.

Range_lookup: this must be FALSE for an exact match

NB: The Table array uses absolute referencing ($) for cells A2 and A8, so the formula can be copied down.

Lookup – What does it look like?

The completed 'Gross Pay Calculation' worksheet will look like this:

	A	B	C	D
1	W/c 02/05/20-9			
2	Employee Name	Hrs	Rate/ hr, £	Gross Pay, £
3	Karen Parsons	39	17.00	663.00
4	Phil Morris	40	15.50	620.00
5	Cam Long	25	14.50	362.50
6	Mariyah Sadiq	31	14.50	449.50
7	Mo Gee	24	14.50	348.00
8	Ben Williams	10	14.50	145.00
9	Anish Bhatt	8	14.50	116.00

…and the formulas within it will look like this:

	A	B	C	D
1	W/c 02/05/20-9			
2	Employee Name	Hrs	Rate/ hr, £	Gross Pay, £
3	Karen Parsons	39	=VLOOKUP(A3,'Wage Rates'!$A$2:$B$8,2,FALSE)	=B3*C3
4	Phil Morris	40	=VLOOKUP(A4,'Wage Rates'!$A$2:$B$8,2,FALSE)	=B4*C4
5	Cam Long	25	=VLOOKUP(A5,'Wage Rates'!$A$2:$B$8,2,FALSE)	=B5*C5
6	Mariyah Sadiq	31	=VLOOKUP(A6,'Wage Rates'!$A$2:$B$8,2,FALSE)	=B6*C6
7	Mo Gee	24	=VLOOKUP(A7,'Wage Rates'!$A$2:$B$8,2,FALSE)	=B7*C7
8	Ben Williams	10	=VLOOKUP(A8,'Wage Rates'!$A$2:$B$8,2,FALSE)	=B8*C8
9	Anish Bhatt	8	=VLOOKUP(A9,'Wage Rates'!$A$2:$B$8,2,FALSE)	=B9*C9

As you can see, the **vlookup** always looks at the same Table array – only the cell the person's name is in is changing (A3, A4, A5, etc).

31 Manipulating data

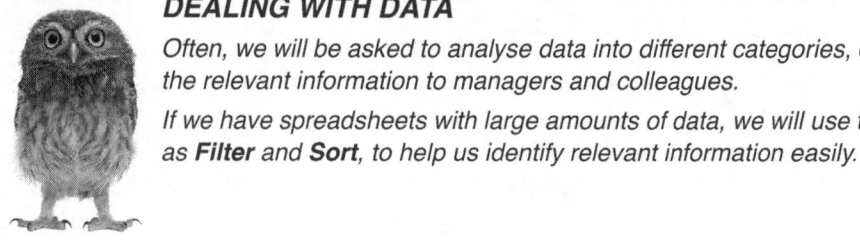

DEALING WITH DATA

Often, we will be asked to analyse data into different categories, only giving the relevant information to managers and colleagues.

*If we have spreadsheets with large amounts of data, we will use tools, such as **Filter** and **Sort**, to help us identify relevant information easily.*

What are Sort and Filter used for?

We could use **Sort** and **Filter** for the following:

- Sorting cost information by behaviour to enable us to produce break-even analysis, using **subtotal** (chapter 29)

- Filtering sales by salesperson, region, product type, as required by management

- Determining the amount of different inventory lines held at year end

Sort – How do you do it?

Highlight all the information, including the headings, that you want to **Sort**.

On the **Data** ribbon, use the **Sort** button:

The box below will appear.

Sort by: the information you want sorted – the column Cost Category here

Sort On: cell values – text or numbers

Order: Z to A, A to Z or you can customise this using the dropdown menu

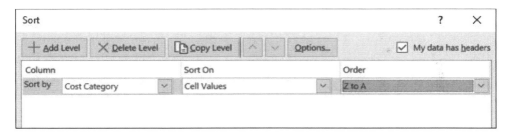

Sort – What does it look like?

Let's use this example, which we want to sort by Cost Category:

	A	B	C
1	**Tom's Nurseries**		
2	**Quarter ended 30 June 20-5**		
3	**Cost Description**	**Cost Category**	**Actual cost**
4	Compost	Variable cost	£16,421
5	Compostable pots	Variable cost	£15,400
6	Depreciation of greenhouses	Fixed cost	£4,700
7	Fixed hire cost plus cost per mile	Semi-variable cost	£6,900
8	Hire of additional temporary greenhouses	Fixed cost	£3,000
9	Plastic pots	Variable cost	£5,600
10	Power (heating greenhouses)	Semi-variable cost	£12,300
11	Rates of nursery	Fixed cost	£11,450
12	Seed costs	Variable cost	£20,432
13	Wages of seed planters and cultivators	Variable cost	£35,498

The cells highlighted to **Sort** would be A3:C13, including the header row, as the 'My data has headers' box is ticked when we do the **Sort** (see previous page).

Once it is sorted it will look like this:

	A	B	C
1	Tom's Nurseries		
2	Quarter ended 30 June 20-5		
3	Cost Description	Cost Category	Actual cost
4	Compost	Variable cost	£16,421
5	Compostable pots	Variable cost	£15,400
6	Plastic pots	Variable cost	£5,600
7	Seed costs	Variable cost	£20,432
8	Wages of seed planters and cultivators	Variable cost	£35,498
9	Fixed hire cost plus cost per mile	Semi-variable cost	£6,900
10	Power (heating greenhouses)	Semi-variable cost	£12,300
11	Depreciation of greenhouses	Fixed cost	£4,700
12	Hire of additional temporary greenhouses	Fixed cost	£3,000
13	Rates of nursery	Fixed cost	£11,450

It is easy to see which costs are in each category. You could then use **subtotal** to add up
the variable, semi-variable and fixed costs.

Filter – How do you do it?

Highlight all the information, including the headings, that you want to **filter**.

On the **Data** ribbon, use the **Filter** button:

This will put an arrow at the top of each column of data in the top right-hand corner, shown here in the Month column.

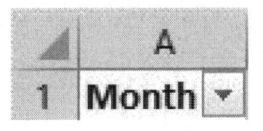

You can then choose to **filter** whatever information you want to in the data you have by clicking on the arrow. The **filter** choices will depend on the data you have – it could be month, product type, region, salesperson, etc.

Let's look at an example to see how the **filter** works.

Filter – What does it look like?

Let's use this example, which we want to **filter** by Region. Clicking on the Region arrow gives you the Filter box, with choices for Midlands and South West.

	A	B	C
1	Month ▾	Region ▾	Value ▾
2	Jan	South West	£65,200
3	Feb	South West	£42,100
4	Feb	Midlands	£57,300
5	Mar	South West	£75,400
6	Jan	Midlands	£47,900
7	Mar	Midlands	£63,200
8	Feb	South West	£49,800

Clicking on the box next to the Region Selects or Unselects it. We just want the Midlands, so the **filter** box, with Midlands selected, will look like the one below on the left, and the information will be filtered accordingly, shown on the right:

	A	B	C
1	Month ▾	Region ▾	Value ▾
4	Feb	Midlands	£57,300
6	Jan	Midlands	£47,900
7	Mar	Midlands	£63,200

A↓ Sort A to Z

Z↓ Sort Z to A

Sort by Color >

Sheet View >

Clear Filter From "Region"

Filter by Color >

Text Filters >

Search 🔍

- ■ (Select All)
- ☑ Midlands
- ☐ South West

You can use multiple filters at the same time – you can see what is being filtered by the changed arrow – see cell B1.

32 Forecasting and 'What if?' analysis (goalseek)

FOCUS ON THE FUTURE...

*Accountants may be asked to predict future materials prices, based on historic information, when producing budgets and the **forecast** function does this perfectly.*

*Part of the budgeting process may also include considering different scenarios. **Goalseek** is a spreadsheet tool that can help us do this effectively.*

What are Forecast and Goalseek used for?

We could use **forecast** for the following:

- Determining how much the price of raw materials is likely to be
- Forecasting sales volumes

and **goalseek** for:

- A required budgeted profit by changing sales volume
- The amount materials must cost to reach a specified unit cost

Forecast – How do you do it?

You will need some data you want to predict. Let's look at forecasting the price of a material we use, PM821. We have six months of data, shown below.

	A	B
1	**Material PM821**	
2	**Period**	**Price per tonne, £**
3	1	65
4	2	67
5	3	66
6	4	69
7	5	71
8	6	74
9	12	

In this example, we want to find the price for Material PM821 in period 12, so we will use the **forecast** function in cell B9 to do so.

The forecast function effectively finds the average increase, based on the data, so using recent data and several months is likely to give the best estimate!

Forecast – How do you do it?

Click in cell B9, on the previous page, and on the Formulas ribbon, use Insert Function to insert **forecast**. The **forecast** function below is completed to find the price of materials for period 12.

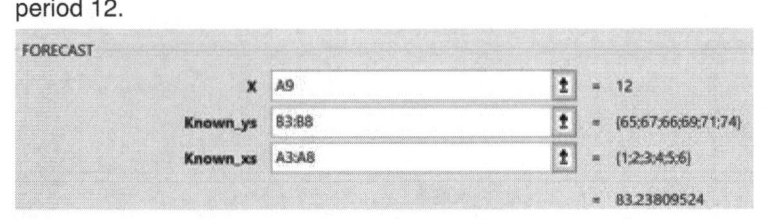

X: the period you want to know the material price of
Known_ys: the known (historic) prices you already have, cells B3:B8
Known_xs: the historic periods, 1-6 here, you already have, cells A3:A8

Forecast – What does it look like?

▲	A	B
1	**Material PM821**	
2	**Period**	**Price per tonne, £**
9	12	83.24

As you can see, the estimate for the price of PM821 is £83.24. Be careful to use the right period when you do the calculation – we have materials' prices here from period 1-6 and want to know about period 12.

Goalseek – How do you do it?

Let's use an example, shown below, where we want to know how many bags of treats we need to sell to earn a profit of £150,000.

◢	A	B	C	D
1	**Miss Molly Pet Treats Ltd**			
2	**Product : Woofily Good Treats**			
3		**Budget for year ending 30 June 20-3**		
4	Bags sold	400,000	550,000	700,000
5	Revenue	£1,000,000	£1,375,000	£1,610,000
6	Total variable costs	£616,000	£847,000	£1,078,000
7	Contribution	£384,000	£528,000	£532,000
8	*Total fixed costs*	*£381,000*	*£381,000*	*£416,000*
9	Forecast profit/ (loss)	£3,000	£147,000	£116,000
10	Price per bag	£2.50	£2.50	£2.30
11	Contribution per bag	£0.96	£0.96	£0.76
12	Forecast profit / (loss)	£0.01	£0.27	£0.17

Goalseek – How do you do it?

It is *very* important to note that the spreadsheet used must include *numbers* and *formulas*. **Goalseek** changes one number to find a required value in another cell. Here, revenue (row 5) and variable costs (row 6) formulas both rely on the number of bags sold, (row 4) less the fixed costs number (row 8) to determine profit. We can change D4, for example, and the forecast profit (D9) will be recalculated correctly.

3		Budget for year ending 30 June 20-3		
4	**Bags sold**	400000	550000	700000
5	**Revenue**	=B4*B10	=C4*C10	=D4*D10
6	Total variable costs	=1.54*B4	=1.54*C4	=1.54*D4
7	**Contribution**	=B5-B6	=C5-C6	=D5-D6
8	*Total fixed costs*	381000	381000	416000
9	**Forecast profit/ (loss)**	=B7-B8	=C7-C8	=D7-D8
10	Price per bag	2.5	2.5	2.3
11	Contribution per bag	=B7/B4	=C7/C4	=D7/D4
12	Forecast profit / (loss) per bag	=B9/B4	=C9/C4	=D9/D4

Goalseek – How do you do it? Cont'd

So, let's say we want to know how many bags we must sell to earn a profit of £150,000, assuming the variable costs stay the same and the fixed costs remain at £416,000 for higher outputs.

Click on the cell you want a specified value in – D9 in this case. On the **Data** ribbon, click on the button below and choose **goalseek**.

Choosing **goalseek** makes the table to the right appear.

You need to fill this in:

Set cell: D9 (the profit)

To value: £150,000

By changing cell: Bags sold, $D$4 (click on the cell to choose it and it will automatically show with absolute referencing).

When complete it looks like this:

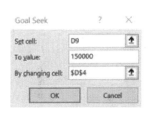

To complete the **goalseek** function click 'OK'.

The spreadsheet will recalculate to find the required bags sold and will look like this.

	A	B	C	D
1	**Miss Molly Pet Treats Ltd**			
2	**Product : Woofily Good Treats**			
3		Budget for year ending 30 June 20-3		
4	**Bags sold**	400,000	550,000	744,737
5	**Revenue**	£1,000,000	£1,375,000	£1,712,895
6	Total variable costs	£616,000	£847,000	£1,146,895
7	**Contribution**	£384,000	£528,000	£566,000
8	*Total fixed costs*	*£381,000*	*£381,000*	*£416,000*
9	**Forecast profit/ (loss)**	**£3,000**	**£147,000**	**£150,000**
10	Price per bag	£2.50	£2.50	£2.30
11	Contribution per bag	£0.96	£0.96	£0.76
12	Forecast profit / (loss) per bag	£0.01	£0.27	£0.20

Goal Seek Status ? ✕

Goal Seeking with Cell D9
found a solution.

Target value: 150000
Current value: £150,000

OK   Cancel

The **goalseek** is complete and the target value and current value match in the 'Goal Seek Status' box. As you can see, we need to sell 744,737 bags to make £150,000 profit (cell D4).

33 Data integrity – protecting cells and data validation

PROTECTING DATA INTEGRITY

*Often a spreadsheet may be updated by non-finance staff, who may accidentally corrupt a spreadsheet. To avoid this, use **protection** on the cells in the worksheet, so only the person who knows the password can change them.*

*Another useful tool is **data validation**, where only a certain supplier, product or customer can be chosen for inclusion in a report, again protecting the integrity or even enforcing the purchasing policy of the business.*

What are protection and data validation used for?

We could use **protection** for the following:

- Protecting wage rates on payroll spreadsheets

- Protecting key formulas in the budgeting spreadsheets, so only variable costs and sales price can be changed

and **data validation** for:

- Placing orders only with approved suppliers
- Entering only valid product codes
- Preventing input errors of figures that are outside the expected range

Protection – How do you do it? Using a 3 step process.....

We use Format cells to do it and are going to use some payroll calculations.

Step 1

'Unlock' all the cells in the worksheet by right clicking on the triangle in the top left-hand corner to highlight the whole sheet.

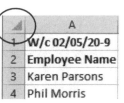

	A
1	W/c 02/05/20-9
2	**Employee Name**
3	Karen Parsons
4	Phil Morris

Choose Format Cells from the menu and highlight it so the box below appears. Choose the Protection tab and click on '**Locked**' to make the tick disappear and press OK. This unlocks (unprotected) every cell.

Protection – How do you do it? Cont'd

Step 2

Highlight the cells you want to protect. We only want the hours information to be changeable in the spreadsheet below, so this is not highlighted.

	A	B	C	D
1	W/c 02/05/20-9			
2	Employee Name	Hrs	Rate/ hr, £	Gross Pay, £
3	Karen Parsons	39	17.00	663.00
4	Phil Morris	40	15.50	620.00
5	Cam Long	25	14.50	362.50
6	Mariyah Sadiq	31	14.50	449.50
7	Mo Gee	24	14.50	348.00
8	Ben Williams	10	14.50	145.00
9	Anish Bhatt	8	14.50	116.00

Right click and bring up Format Cells again. This time, click the '***Locked***' box so it has a tick showing '***Locked***' then click 'OK'. When you have protected the worksheet all the highlighted cells will be locked i.e. cannot be changed.

Step 3

You can now protect the worksheet. The cells can be changed until this is done. On the **Review** ribbon, choose **Protect sheet** to get to the menu below.

Make sure you choose the correct option: in this case we want users to Select unlocked cells only, so this box is ticked.

You can use a password to protect the worksheet, but make sure you keep a note of this – without it the worksheet will remain protected, and the cells locked, forever!

Protection – What does it look like?

The spreadsheet looks no different, but if your move your cursor onto any locked cells, you cannot choose them or go into them. So we can amend cell B5, shown highlighted below, but cannot amend D5, for example.

	A	B	C	D
1	W/c 02/05/20-9			
2	Employee Name	Hrs	Rate/ hr, £	Gross Pay, £
3	Karen Parsons	39	17.00	663.00
4	Phil Morris	40	15.50	620.00
5	Cam Long	25	14.50	362.50
6	Mariyah Sadiq	31	14.50	449.50
7	Mo Gee	24	14.50	348.00
8	Ben Williams	10	14.50	145.00
9	Anish Bhatt	8	14.50	116.00

You can unprotect the sheet by using the Review ribbon and Unprotect sheet…as long as you have remembered the password!

Data validation – How do you do it?

This tool will allow you to only enter specified data into certain cells. We want to only have approved suppliers for purchasing goods for Any Weather Barbeques Ltd entered into B4:B9 in the example below:

	A	B	C	D	E
1	Any Weather Barbeques Ltd			Approved Supplier	
2	Purchase orders for May 20X2			BC Coatings Ltd	
3	Material	Supplier		LP Handles Ltd	
4	Enamel coatings			Metal Supplies Ltd	
5	Aluminium			Weatherproof Fabrics Ltd	
6	Steel				
7	Chrome				
8	Fabric covers				
9	Handles				

First highlight B4:B9, then find **data validation** on the Data ribbon on the toolbar.

Data validation – How do you do it? Cont'd

Choose **data validation** and this box appears:

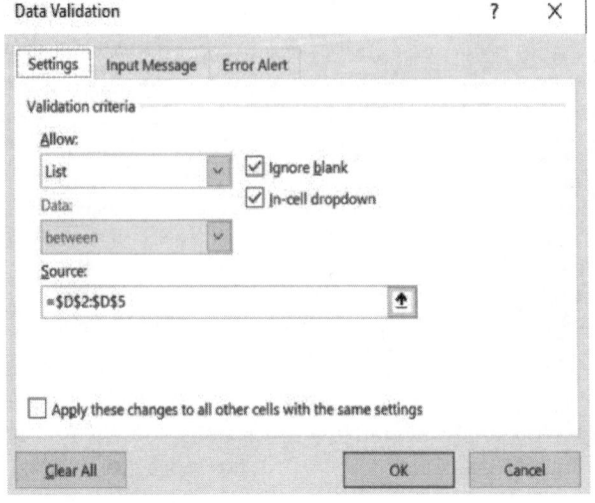

Allow: use this to set the criteria, in this case a list. There are several other options to restrict data entry.

Data: can be used to restrict the range of data entered to certain limits.

Source: this is where the approved suppliers you want to choose from are for the example, =$D$2:$D$5.

You can add an 'Input Message' and 'Error Alert' to prompt users by clicking on the other tabs.

Once completed, click 'OK'.

Data validation – What does it look like?

In the chosen cells, you will have a dropdown menu that only allows you to choose specified items – in this case specified suppliers.

	A	B	C
1	**Any Weather Barbeques Ltd**		
2	**Purchase orders for May 20X2**		
3	**Material**	**Supplier**	
4	Enamel coatings	BC Coatings Ltd	
5	Aluminium	Metal Supplies Ltd	
6	Steel	Metal Supplies Ltd	
7	Chrome	Metal Supplies Ltd	
8	Fabric covers		
9	Handles	BC Coatings Ltd	
10		LP Handles Ltd	
11		Metal Supplies Ltd	
		Weatherproof Fabrics Ltd	

34 Auditing tools

IS THE FORMULA RIGHT?

*Spreadsheets can sometimes get quite complicated and, consequently, it may be useful to determine which cells are included in a formula. This can be done in several ways including **trace precedents**, **trace dependents** and **show formulas**.*

What are trace precedents and dependents and show formulas used for?

We could use **trace precedents** and **trace dependents** for:

■ Visually seeing the cells feeding into a budget or being used on an extended trial balance to help us spot errors

We use **show formulas** to:

■ Highlight how we have arrived at a figure – a budgeted profit, sales commission, gross pay – to identify errors or show how it has been calculated. Again, this will help us spot errors or for training staff

Tracing precedents, dependents and showing formulas – How do you do it?

The two trace functions use arrows to show what is included in the formula in a cell **(trace precedents)** or the cell it is then included in **(trace dependents)**.

On the Formulas ribbon on the toolbar, use the Formula Auditing section:

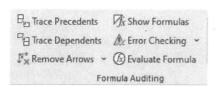

Click on a cell and then click on either 'Trace Precedents' or 'Trace Dependents'. Arrows appear showing the cells the chosen cell is linked to, either heading to it (precedents) or away from it (dependents).

By clicking on 'Show Formulas', the spreadsheet reveals every formula used on the worksheet in each cell. You may have to alter the column sizes to see all of it. To hide the formulas, click this choice again.

Let's use it on the **goalseek** example on page 160. We want to find the precedents of the forecast profit in cell D9, to make sure it is including 'Contribution' and 'Total fixed costs'. We then want to see if it is included in the forecast profit per bag.

Tracing precedents, dependents – What does it look like?

Once we highlight D9 and choose both **trace precedents** and **trace dependents**, this is what happens:

	A	B	C	D
1	**Miss Molly Pet Treats Ltd**			
2	**Product : Woofily Good Treats**			
3	**Budget for year ending 30 June 20-3**			
4	Bags sold	400,000	550,000	700,000
5	Revenue	£1,000,000	£1,375,000	£1,610,000
6	Total variable costs	£616,000	£847,000	£1,078,000
7	Contribution	£384,000	£528,000	£532,000
8	*Total fixed costs*	*£381,000*	*£381,000*	*£416,000*
9	Forecast profit/ (loss)	£3,000	£147,000	£116,000
10	Price per bag	£2.50	£2.50	£2.30
11	Contribution per bag	£0.96	£0.96	£0.76
12	Forecast profit / (loss) per bag	£0.01	£0.27	£0.17

The arrows show the cells included in the formula in D9 (D7 & D8) and which cells use D9 (D12).

Show formulas – What does it look like?

This reveals the formulas used on the whole sheet.

3		Budget for year ending 30 June 20-3		
4	**Bags sold**	**400000**	**550000**	**700000**
5	**Revenue**	**=B4*B10**	**=C4*C10**	**=D4*D10**
6	Total variable costs	=1.54*B4	=1.54*C4	=1.54*D4
7	**Contribution**	**=B5-B6**	**=C5-C6**	**=D5-D6**
8	*Total fixed costs*	*381000*	*381000*	*416000*
9	**Forecast profit/ (loss)**	**=B7-B8**	**=C7-C8**	**=D7-D8**
10	Price per bag	2.5	2.5	2.3
11	Contribution per bag	=B7/B4	=C7/C4	=D7/D4
12	Forecast profit / (loss) per	=B9/B4	=C9/C4	=D9/D4

Note: numbers are shown as numbers (without formatting) and the formulas as cell references or multiplied by a number, etc.

35 Creating charts

WHEN PICTURES MAKE SENSE

Financial information can be challenging to understand for non-financial managers, so charts and graphs (Excel calls them all charts) are useful tools to make this more understandable.

Different types of chart can be used to show information in a variety of ways. The possibilities are endless....

What are charts used for?

We could use **charts** for:

- Plotting sales against this year, last year or budget
- Showing how expenses are spent in a business
- Informing production of under- or over-spend on production
- Comparing budgeted and actual staff costs

…..and many more!

Creating charts – How do you do it?

First select the data set you want to plot, then use the chart wizard to help you. On the Insert ribbon on the Toolbar use the Charts section to insert a chart:

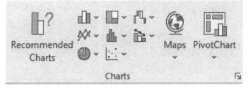

Click on the type of chart you want, by clicking on the arrow by the side of each chart. The choices include:

■ 2-D or 3-D column (vertical lines) or bar (horizontal lines), including stacked charts (where elements add on top of one another)

■ Line charts

■ Pie (circular) charts either filled in or like a doughnut

Often selecting the 'Recommended Charts' will show suitable options. This will automatically show data in different colours and add a key (legend) to the chart, showing what each colour represents and a box for the Chart Title.

Creating charts – How do you do it?

Let's create a clustered chart for this data for a business selling beds.

	A	B	C
1	Year ended 31 March 20-6		
2		Actual Sales	Budgeted Sales
3	Dreamy	£297,800	£315,840
4	Cosy	£370,800	£354,890
5	Dreamy City	£672,550	£614,800
6	Sleepy	£339,800	£389,600
7	Cosy City	£257,600	£231,400
8	Sleep City	£97,450	£142,800
9	Nest	£325,350	£256,400
10	Cosset	£319,250	£341,600
11	Nest City	£294,000	£305,400

The data selected includes the headings, A2:A11, so when created, the chart will automatically include these.

Using the Recommended Charts button brings examples of charts, so we can pick the one we want.

Select a recommended chart, by clicking on it, and a chart will automatically be produced on the same worksheet – see below.

In the Toolbar, a Chart Design ribbon is now available.

Sales – Actual vs Budget
Year ended 31 March 20-6

- The vertical (y axis) shows the **data series** (sales)
- The horizontal (x axis) shows the **category** (type of bed sold)
- The **legend** shows Actual sales and Budgeted sales, so you know which colour is which. This is at the bottom of the graph
- The **scale** (range of values) on the y axis is £100,000. The x axis can have a scale too, depending on the graph

  Clicking on the chart allows us to edit the Chart title: Sales – Actual vs Budget Year ended 31 March 20-6

Clicking on the Chart Design ribbon allows us to change many features of the chart, including adding new chart elements using the dropdown arrow, indicated below:

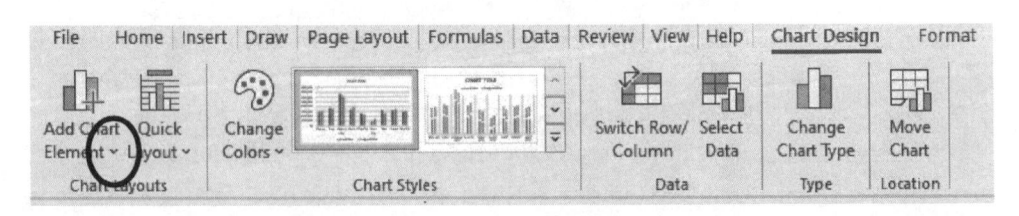

Depending on your version of Excel, clicking on the chart may cause a shortcut to Chart Design editing to appear in the top right-hand corner.

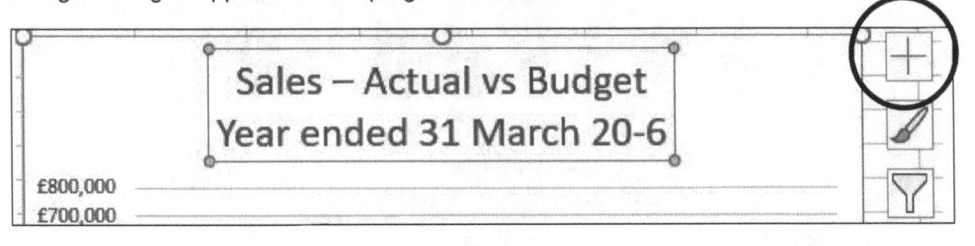

Creating charts – how do you do this?

You can amend the Chart Elements using this menu:

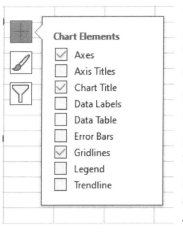

Axes: change the scale, font, number format, etc.

Axis title: can be added if wanted and formatted as required.

Chart titles: can be amended and formatted.

Data labels: can be added to each data set to show the individual number being plotted.

Data table: can be added to the chart, so the numbers for the data can be seen.

Legend: otherwise known as the key, can be formatted and positioned as desired.

Trendline: can be added if required.

The funnel icon (filter) allows you to remove certain categories if you wish, simply by clicking on it and 'unticking', or deselecting those categories you do not want.

Creating charts – what does it look like?

This is the original chart, with some chart elements amended.

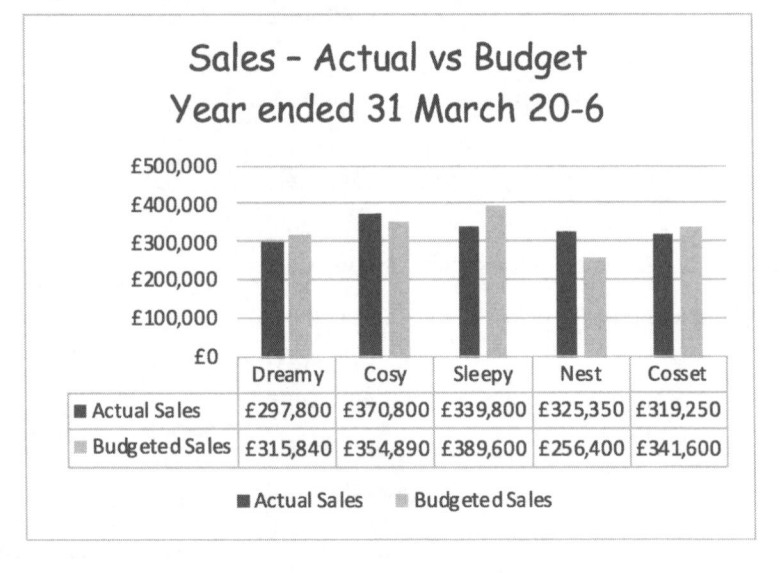

	Dreamy	Cosy	Sleepy	Nest	Cosset
■ Actual Sales	£297,800	£370,800	£339,800	£325,350	£319,250
■ Budgeted Sales	£315,840	£354,890	£389,600	£256,400	£341,600

Sales – Actual vs Budget
Year ended 31 March 20-6

■ Actual Sales   ■ Budgeted Sales

The amended chart elements are:

- The categories have been filtered to remove any City products
- The title font and size have been changed
- The graph has been stretched by clicking on it and pulling it, as you would a picture, to make the differences between actual and budget clearer
- Data table has been added
- The colour of Budget Sales has changed. You can do this by clicking on the column and the Format Data Series menu appears:

    This menu allows you to change the look of the information, to make the graph even more accessible.

36 Amending charts

ALL CHANGE!

Charts are useful tools and, inevitably, will need to be changed to include new data or shown in a different style for new managers or employees. You need to be able to amend data included in a chart, as well as the chart type. Amending axis scales, fonts, etc can be done using the Chart Elements menus, from the previous chapter.

How do you amend data and chart types?

Using the Chart Design ribbon makes it easy to change chart type or the data:

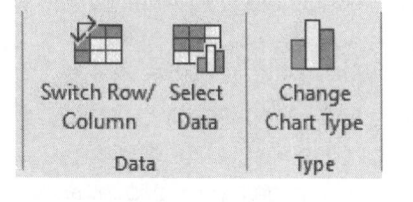

Click 'Select Data' to bring up the box below, so you can add, edit and remove data from the chart.

You can also choose 'Change Chart Type' and experiment to choose the one you like best.

Amended data and chart types – what do they look like?

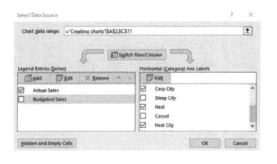

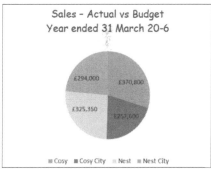

Only the Actual Sales for the City ranges are included on the chart which is now a 2D pie chart.

37 Pivot tables and charts

DEALING WITH LOTS OF DATA

Pivot tables *and **pivot charts** can be used to summarise large tables of data into useful reports for managers.*

*Often **pivot tables** and **pivot charts** go together, so you can amend the chart very quickly – again a useful facility.*

What are pivot tables and pivot charts used for?

Examples include:

- Reporting on sales by product per month, by location
- Inventory type, held at certain locations
- Categorising costs for products and by type

Pivot tables and pivot charts – how do you do them?

We can use the Insert ribbon on the toolbar and select the following:

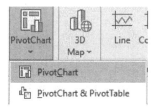

Insert either a Pivot Chart, Pivot Chart and Pivot Table or Pivot Table by choosing the required option from one of the two menus.

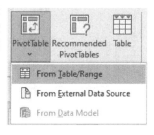

We are going to produce a **pivot table** using the data on the next page for a bed manufacturer.

Pivot tables and pivot charts – how do you do them? Cont'd

First, select the data you want to summarise including headings – in this example A1:E14 is highlighted.

	A	B	C	D	E
1	Item number	Type	Description	Quantity Sold	When
2	8475	Cosy SK	Oatmeal Super King size	23	April
3	8472	Cosy D	Oatmeal Double	81	April
4	8471	Cosy S	Oatmeal Single	37	March
5	6960	Dreamy City Q	Grey Queen size	79	April
6	9330	Cosset SK	Kashmir Super King size	67	March
7	9326	Cosset S	Kashmir Single	42	March
8	9330	Cosset SK	Kashmir Super King size	74	February
9	9329	Cosset K	Kashmir King size	23	February
10	8472	Cosy D	Oatmeal Double	53	February
11	6961	Dreamy City K	Grey King size	27	February
12	6960	Dreamy City Q	Grey Queen size	84	February
13	6958	Dreamy City S	Grey Single	23	February
14	8473	Cosy Q	Oatmeal Queen size	65	March

Then, to insert a **pivot table**, select this from the Insert, PivotTable menu and this box appears:

You can choose for the pivot table to appear in a new worksheet (shown here) or the original sheet.

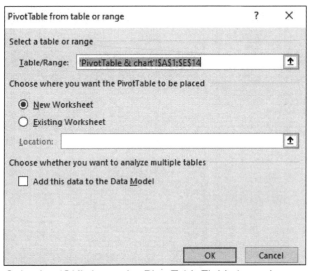

PivotTable from table or range	?	×

Select a table or range

Table/Range: 'PivotTable & chart'!$A$1:$E$14   ⬆

Choose where you want the PivotTable to be placed

● New Worksheet

○ Existing Worksheet

Location: ⬆

Choose whether you want to analyze multiple tables

☐ Add this data to the Data Model

OK   Cancel

Selecting 'OK' shows the PivotTableFields box, shown on the next page:

Pivot tables and pivot charts – how do you do them? Cont'd

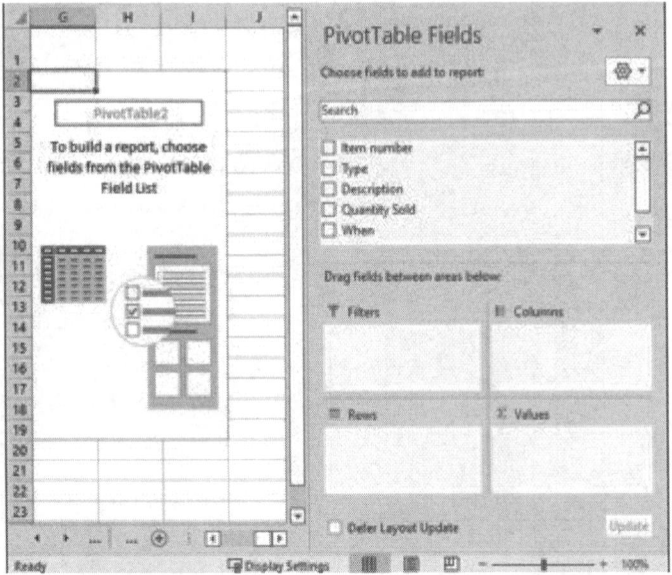

You now tick the information (field) you want, then drag and drop the information into one of the four quadrants in the bottom half of the shaded box.

Fields should be dropped into either Columns or Rows and the numerical data dropped into Values. Your pivot table will appear instantly, showing the summarised data.

Pivot table – what does it look like?

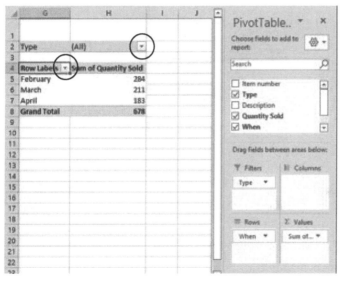

The Type field has been dropped into the Filters quadrant so that the data can be filtered by type.

The data can also be filtered by When as there is an arrow above this field.

The quantity sold has been summed (totalled) but there are many other options.

Pivot chart – how do you do it?

Using the same data as before, Insert Pivot Chart and choose a chart type.

The data fields and filters work in the same way, and a 2D bar chart is created:

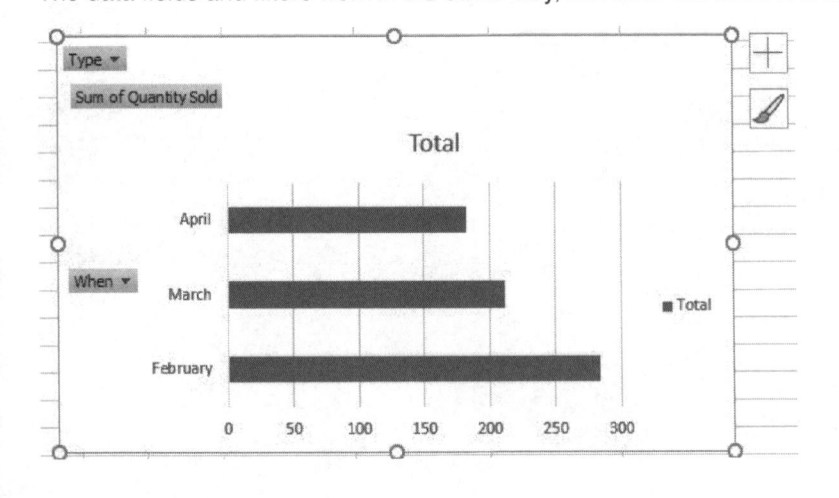

Pivot chart – what does it look like?

We can amend the chart elements in the same way as normal charts, so we have changed the colours. The new chart has two arrows, so we can amend the chart to include the Type and When it was sold. If we just want products, excluding City, sold in the period, we can do this by filtering using Type, highlighted below, and the following graph will be produced.

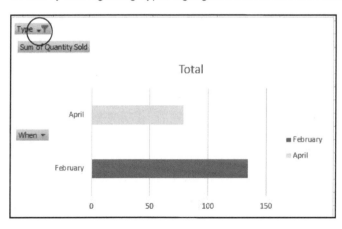

38 Memory aids

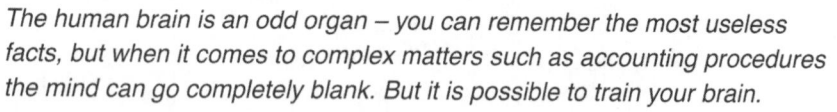

KEEPING YOUR MEMORY FIT

The human brain is an odd organ – you can remember the most useless facts, but when it comes to complex matters such as accounting procedures the mind can go completely blank. But it is possible to train your brain.

At the beginning of this Guide there are some revision tips which suggest that you can study effectively and recall information by . . .

- **Observing**, ie remembering what information looks like on the page, using diagrams, lists, mind-maps and colour coding. Memory is very visual.

- **Writing** information down, using flash cards, post-it notes, notes on a phone. It is the actual process of writing which helps to fix the information in the brain.

- **Learning** by regularly going through your course notes and text books. Find a 'study buddy' in your class (or online) to teach and test each other as the course progresses.

- **Chill out** when you get tired. Give your brain a chance to recover. Get some exercise and fresh air, work out. In the ancient world there was the saying that a fit body was usually home to a fit mind.

- **Treats** – promise yourself rewards when you have finished studying – meet friends, eat chocolate, have a drink, listen to music.

exam preparation

- **Practice, practice, practice** when preparing for your assessment.

  Practice the questions and assessments in the Osborne Books workbooks.

  Practice the free online assessments on the Osborne Books website:

  Log on to www.osbornebooks.co.uk/elearning

using the memory aids

On the next few pages are blank spaces for you to set out ways of remembering many of the definitions and formulas needed for your AAT assessment.

managing materials inventory

Enter in the blank spaces definitions of the terms in the left-hand column.

inventory buffer	
lead time	
re-order level	
re-order quantity	

costing methods

Enter in the blank spaces examples of organisations which are likely to use the costing methods listed on the left.

unit costing	
job costing	
batch costing	
service costing	
process costing	

cost apportionment

Enter in each of the blank spaces appropriate ways to apportion between responsibility centres the indirect costs listed on the left.

factory rent	
depreciation of machinery	
power for machinery	
factory heating	
canteen costs	

break-even analysis

Enter in each of the blank spaces the formulas for the terms listed on the left.

contribution	
profit/volume (contribution/sales) ratio	
break-even (units)	
margin of safety (units)	
margin of safety (% of budgeted sales)	

resources ratios

Enter in the blank spaces formulas of the ratios in the left-hand column.

inventory holding period (days)	
trade receivables collection period (days)	
trade payables payment period (days)	
working capital cycle (days)	

index